100 Great Ideas *to* Relax and Reduce Stress

Tyndale House Publishers, Inc.

Carol Stream, Illinois

Visit Tyndale's exciting Web site at www.tyndale.com.

TYNDALE and Tyndale's quill logo are registered trademarks of Tyndale House Publishers, Inc.

100 Great Ideas to Relax and Reduce Stress
Copyright © 2010 by GRQ, Inc. All rights reserved.

Editor: Lila Empson Wavering
Manuscript written and compiled by Snapdragon Group℠
Design: Whisner Design Group

Library of Congress Cataloging-in-Publication Data

100 great ideas to relax and reduce stress / [manuscript written and compiled by Snapdragon GroupSM].
    p. cm.
 ISBN 978-1-4143-3887-3 (sc)
 1. Stress (Psychology)--Religious aspects--Christianity. 2. Stress management--Religious aspects--Christianity. I. Snapdragon Group (Tulsa, Okla.)
 BV4509.5.A16 2010
 248.8′6--dc22

2010017312

Printed in the United States of America

16 15 14 13 12 11
 7 6 5 4 3

If you are tired from carrying heavy burdens,
come to me and I will give you rest.

Matthew 11:28, CEV

Don't let your mind bully your body into believing
it must carry the burden of its worries.

Astrid Alauda

Give your stress wings and let it fly away.

Terri Guillemets

Sometimes a headache is all in your head. Relax.

Hartman Jule

You will keep in perfect peace all who trust in you,
all whose thoughts are fixed on you!

Isaiah 26:3, NLT

Contents

Introduction

The Power of Prayer

Overcoming Perfectionism

Contents continued

Reaching Out to Others

Positive Thinking

Contents continued

Contents continued

Don't worry about anything; instead, pray about everything.
Tell God what you need, and thank him for all he has done.

Philippians 4:6, NLT

Do not lose your inward peace for anything whatsoever,
even if your whole world seems upset.

Saint Francis de Sales

There is a calmness to a life lived in gratitude, a quiet joy.

Ralph H. Blum

It is requisite for the relaxation of the mind that we
make use, from time to time, of playful deeds and jokes.

Saint Thomas Aquinas

Cast all your anxiety on him because he cares for you.

1 Peter 5:7, NIV

Introduction

If you are distressed by anything external, the pain is not due to the thing itself,
but to your estimate of it; and this you have the power to revoke at any moment.

Marcus Aurelius

Stress is a highly subjective phenomenon that differs in intensity and physical and emotional response with each person. While researchers find it difficult to define, they agree it is one of the greatest health risks in our society. It's difficult to think of any disease or condition, physical, mental, or emotional, that is not aggravated by stress. Your doctor can do little to help, except, perhaps, prescribe an extended stay in the Himalayas! It's up to you to examine your lifestyle and find ways to protect the mind and body God gave you.

Because being stress-free seems to be impossible, it is important that we all have active strategies for keeping personal stress under control. That is why *100 Great Ideas to Relax and Reduce Stress* was written. In the pages of this book, you will find simple, doable, inexpensive ideas that can help bring your stress level down, help you relax, and help improve your physical, emotional, mental, and even spiritual health.

You may not be able to eliminate stressful circumstances from your life or prescribe how your body will respond to those stressors, but you need not live on the cusp of a raging internal volcano. There are things you can do, and we pray that this book will help you learn effective ways to let off steam and relax enough to bring joy and satisfaction back into your everyday life.

The greatest weapon against stress is our ability to choose one thought over another.
WILLIAM JAMES

1   Treat Yourself to a Good Laugh

Does it sometimes feel as if you got up on the wrong side of the bed? Everything is bugging you, and your nerves are on edge. Then you hear something that tickles your funny bone, and just like that your whole outlook changes. Laughter really is the best medicine.

Think about how you feel after a hearty laugh. It doesn't change your circumstances; it changes only the way you view them. Your muscles relax, and tension slips away. Laughter lowers blood pressure, strengthens the immune system, and promotes heart health. Without a doubt, when God gave you the ability to laugh, he gave you an incredible tool to help you release inner stress and calm your body and mind. But that's just the beginning. Sharing a laugh with another person can enhance your relationship, strengthen your bond, and even defuse a quarrel.

Be ready for laughter by keeping a smile on your face and gratitude for God's blessings in your heart. Cultivate the company of joyful people. Choose to celebrate the lighter side of life, and share a generous dose of your laughter with others.

The cheerful heart has a continual feast.

Proverbs 15:15, NIV

Call to mind what is causing you stress today. Now describe the situation in humorous terms. Exaggerate if you want to. Be outrageous. Allow yourself to laugh at the situation and feel the relief.

Breathe as If You Mean It

2

Lean back, relax, and put your body at rest. As your breathing becomes controlled and unhurried, your throat, neck, and shoulders loosen and your mind opens to pleasant, peaceful thoughts and images.

Most people pay little attention to their breathing, and yet how you breathe makes a big difference in the way you feel. In a stressful situation, a few slow, deep breaths can boost your body's oxygen supply and help you regain control of your physical and emotional responses. In addition, the few seconds you spend in mindful breathing let you mentally step away from the cause of your stress, allowing you to return with a clearer head and a more balanced perspective.

Your breath is God's gift of life. Each day, spend a minute concentrating on nothing but the miracle of being able to breathe. Inhale and exhale calmly and rhythmically, and pay attention to how breathing feels and sounds. Take deep, full breaths, and drink in the power of your breaths to cover yourself with serenity and peace.

The LORD God formed the man from the dust of the ground. He breathed the breath of life into the man's nostrils.

Genesis 2:7, NLT

❧

Take a deep breath through your nose, counting to five as you inhale. Hold your breath for a count of five, and then exhale for a count of ten through your mouth. Repeat this cleansing breath three times, gradually increasing the count as you inhale, hold, and exhale.

13

3

Learn to Say No

It feels good to say yes, and saying no seems selfish. You'd like to help everyone who asks you, but realistically you can't. Forgetting that you are just one person can take a wicked toll on your family, your emotions, and your physical well-being. Sometimes a simple "No, I'm sorry, but I can't manage it" is exactly the right answer.

Sure, your saying no will disappoint a few people, but it will also force them to discover gifts and talents in others. You've never been one to hog the spotlight, and your intentions have always been good. Know that God always has a plan, and that plan usually involves spreading the work around and giving everyone a chance to shine.

Reduce your inner stress by sweetly and graciously saying no when you find it appropriate to do so. Send up a prayer that God will provide just the right person to accomplish the task. That will free you to embrace the yeses in your life with true pleasure and peace of mind.

*One cannot collect
all the beautiful shells
on the beach.*

Anne Morrow
Lindbergh

*When asked to take on any task or project, ask for some
time to think and pray about it. That will allow you to
step past the impulse to say yes and ensure that the things
you do agree to tackle are just right for you.*

14

Unclutter Your Life

4

How many times have you thought about stepping off the treadmill and out of the rat race, leaving behind all that clamoring for money and possessions? The very things that are supposed to make your life easier seem to complicate it instead. But what does leading a simple life really mean? Giving away your possessions? Downsizing? Spending less?

The first logical step to a simpler lifestyle is to deal with what you already have. That's where most of the stress comes from anyway. Start by evaluating your weekly activities. Which ones were once fun but now seem like chores? Go ahead and cut those without feeling guilty. Next, ask yourself if the vacation home has become a burden, if you have too many cars, if you really need all the things filling your closets and kitchen cupboards.

You should keep what you still hold dear, of course, but if something no longer matters, let it go to bless someone else. Own what you have; don't let what you have own you.

A man's life does not consist in the abundance of his possessions.

Luke 12:15, NIV

Say good-bye to impulse purchases, both big and small. Determine not to buy anything the first time you see it. Give yourself time to forget about it. If you do, you didn't really want it in the first place.

5

Look on the Bright Side

God causes everything to work together for the good of those who love God and are called according to his purpose for them.

Romans 8:28, NLT

Do friends call you a pessimist and a worrywart even though you think of yourself as just a realist? "I'm just a glass-half-empty kind of person," you tell them. Unfortunately, your pessimistic perspective has a downside your optimistic friends don't have to deal with. Consistently viewing things from a negative angle can seriously compromise your health, your relationships, and your enjoyment of life. The question you have to ask is, Why live in the dark when you can bask in the light?

Fortunately, there's a cure for pessimism. You can cure the negative thoughts and expectations you have for people and situations. The cure is faith, the kind of faith that trusts in the goodness and veracity of God. While negative thoughts pull you down, faith builds you up. Faith replaces stress and anxiety with hope.

As you actively choose to look on the bright side, a new habit will be formed. One day you'll hear yourself say, "I can't help it. I'm just a glass-half-full kind of person."

Recall a time you thought all was lost. How did you make it through to the other side? Did your faith in God get you there? When you feel yourself slipping into negativity, recall the details of that positive outcome.

Look for Positive People 6

A new project can be so exciting that you are eager to tell your friend all about it. As soon as you've finished talking, however, your friend starts ticking off reasons why your project is doomed. You're left feeling deflated, anxious, and unsure of yourself. There will be stress enough in completing a challenging project. It's best to surround yourself with people who can see and appreciate what you are trying to do. Keep company with those who share your vision and have faith in your talents and abilities.

Positive people are essential to your success, even if they can't add to the technical aspects of the project. When there are breaks in the action, seek out people who possess a light and happy attitude, people who will help recharge your batteries and renew your enthusiasm.

Being positive and being realistic are not mutually exclusive characteristics. You need people who can give you an honest evaluation of your project with a positive spin. You need people who can see the beauty in what you're doing and inspire you to stay on point.

Attitude is a little thing that makes a big difference.

Winston Churchill

If someone you know and love is a negative person, mentally prepare for your times together. Keep the conversation as upbeat as possible, and follow those encounters with visits with two of your most optimistic friends.

17

7

Mean What You Say

The school was having a fund-raiser, and you quickly agreed to help. A coworker undertook a project, and in a cursory gesture of goodwill you offered to help. You didn't take those obligations seriously or stop to consider whether you had the time or the skills to do them. Now you're stressed because someone is asking you to make good on what you said you would do.

It's stressful for you when someone lets you down. It's also stressful for you when you realize too late that you made a promise you can't keep. Relationships can be harmed, and a flurry of explanations and apologies always seems like too little too late.

In the Bible, God has made many promises to you, and each one comes with a stress-free guarantee—his promises will never be broken because he has what it takes to back them up. You aren't God, but you can emulate him by promising only what you know you can deliver.

The LORD always keeps his promises; he is gracious in all he does.

Psalm 145:13, NLT

When someone asks you to make a commitment, promise to think about it. Give yourself time to see if it fits within the context of the other obligations that fill your schedule. It's better to be honest at the beginning than apologetic at the end.

Say What You Mean

8

Maybe your spouse owes you an apology, or maybe you'd like your child to take better care of his room. You could just spell it out for them, but instead you decide on a more subtle approach, which might include meaningful looks, sighs, broad hints, or pouting. At this point, you've stopped communicating and started playing a game called "guess what's bugging me."

Playing games won't get you a satisfactory outcome. Playing games will cause stress to build up inside until you blow up in anger and frustration. The Bible suggests a better approach: simply say what you need to say, and say it in a loving way. How the other person responds is not something you can predict, but at least the other person won't have to guess where you stand on the issue.

Saying what you mean puts the ball in the other person's court and does so without angry words, which can cause collateral damage to the relationship. When in doubt, use your words.

From the opening of my lips will come right things.

Proverbs 8:6, NKJV

When you just can't seem to put your thoughts into words, write them down first. This will give you an opportunity to choose your words more carefully and refine any ambiguities before you speak.

9   Break Big Jobs into Small Pieces

I can do all things through Christ who strengthens me.

Philippians 4:13, NKJV

This is the day you've been dreading. Today you have to tackle that giant project you've been putting off. You sit there wondering where to begin, and your stress level goes into hyperdrive. If you find yourself in this dilemma, follow this sage advice: the best way to move a mountain is to chip away at it one wheelbarrow full of rocks at a time.

The same is true for your mountainous project. Break it down into smaller, more manageable pieces. Spring cleaning? Tackle it one room, one closet, one task at a time. Writing a report for the boss? Gather data, create an outline, write the draft, and so forth. Thank God, and congratulate yourself as you complete each task.

This strategy has proved effective in many aspects of life. Losing weight, overcoming addiction, and raising children are most often successful when viewed in small, daily, even hourly victories. Why stress out when you can get the job done one wheelbarrow-full at a time?

Choose a project you've been putting off. On paper, list the tasks that need to be done in order to complete the project. Choose start and finish dates, and schedule the tasks as evenly as possible between those dates.

Hug Often, Hug Tight

10

Aunt Gracie is in town, and one thing you know for sure—a hugging frenzy is in your future. Your sweet auntie is a hugger extraordinaire and the picture of joyful peace and calm. No jangled nerves for her. Is it really hugging that makes the difference? you ask yourself. In all probability it is.

A study at the University of North Carolina concluded that hugging increases a bonding hormone called oxytocin, while decreasing blood pressure and levels of the stress hormone cortisol in women. Hand-holding was shown to have a similar effect. And guess what else? Both are free.

God created you with an undeniable need to be touched, to feel the physical chemistry of connectedness between yourself and another person. Give and receive as many hugs as possible from your friends and loved ones, especially your dear aunt Gracie. Fairly soon, word will get out that you're a hugger, and other huggers will begin to seek you out. Goodbye, stress.

A hug is like a boomerang—you get it back right away.

Bil Keane

Occasionally you will meet someone who isn't comfortable with being hugged. It's best to respect personal boundaries. Instead, hug that person with your words by offering a personal compliment or encouraging remark.

11

Let Yourself off the Hook

Because of the LORD's great love we are not consumed, for his compassions never fail. They are new every morning; great is your faithfulness.

Lamentations 3:22-23,
NIV

The mistake you just made is a big one. You've replayed it repeatedly in your mind. All those involved have given you their forgiveness, but you can't forgive yourself. You thought you'd get past it eventually, but the big knot of stress in the pit of your stomach has grown bigger rather than smaller. You feel that you probably deserve to feel bad.

The truth is, you do deserve to feel bad. You deserve everything that comes your way as a result of your blunder. But, and this is a big *but*, God intervened on your behalf. He paid your ticket and let you off scot-free.

Now God is asking you to let yourself off the hook. Open your heart, and let the guilt and regret flow out of you. As you embrace the forgiveness you've been offered, you'll feel that big stress knot in the pit of your stomach melt away. You'll open your eyes to find that the sun has risen on a brand-new morning.

Write a thank-you note to God expressing your gratitude for his gift of forgiveness. Tell him about your decision to forgive yourself, and thank him for giving you a chance to begin again.

Turn Off the Voice in Your Head 12

One of the terms for that voice in your head is *self-talk*. It can be a good thing if you're trying to stay pumped for some daunting endeavor. That voice is even a tool to help you sort through a problem. But that's true only if that voice is building you up rather than pulling you down. The voice in your head is often linked to an unfortunate memory or trauma. Sometimes it restates old criticisms and hurtful remarks. Just when you begin to relax, there it is, telling you you're no good.

Understand this. You don't have to put up with that voice. Really, it's nothing more than a recording of negative things you've been told over time. God gave you authority over your mind. You have the power to tape over that negative voice.

Each time you hear that voice click on, preempt it with some God-talk. Remind yourself that you are loved by God, you are his glorious creation, and you are made in his image. Then sit back and relax in the wonder of your new awareness.

Blessed be the LORD,
for he has wondrously
shown his steadfast
love to me.

Psalm 31:21, NRSV

As you work to record a new, positive voice, state your positive affirmations aloud. Hearing the words as you say them will imbue them with more power. After they are firmly established, you can simply close your eyes and listen.

The Power of Prayer

*The most powerful tool available to you in your quest to de-stress your
life is prayer. Not only does prayer provide the opportunity to slow down and
gain perspective, but it also serves as the invitation to release burdens
to God, who ultimately is able to help you resolve them.*

The lives of early Christians were packed with stress. Christians were constantly in danger. They were at odds with their Roman rulers and persecuted even by the religious superstructures around them. Many were killed, and others hid in catacombs under the city in order to avoid arrest. Their belongings were confiscated, they were beaten, and yet, through prayer and constant faith, they persevered.

You probably never will have to live under such dire conditions or endure the stressful situations they encountered. Just the same, when the weight of your circumstances comes to bear, you have access to the same tool that worked so well for them. You can pray.

Prayer, which is simply conversation with God, has many beneficial aspects. Through meditative prayer, you can take the focus from your stressful circumstance and put it on the goodness of God and the blessings he has placed in your life. In prayers of praise and thanksgiving, you can extol God's greatness and his power over your problems. In prayers of petition, you can share your requests and your burdens with him and fully expect his intervention. Replace your worry and anxiety with prayer, and your stress level will begin to decrease immediately.

Top Ten Things to Do

10. Learn to pray right where you are.

9. Talk to God as you would to a friend.

8. Don't hold back; God won't tell anyone.

7. Be truthful; God sees your heart anyway.

6. Confess your sins, and then let them go.

5. Take time to listen.

4. Become aware of God's constant presence.

3. Find opportunities to pray with others.

2. Believe that God hears you.

1. Put your trust in God's goodness.

13   Think before You Speak

Let no one despise your youth, but set the believers an example in speech and conduct, in love, in faith, in purity.

1 Timothy 4:12, NRSV

Oops! You wish a Delete key came with your mouth. You said something you shouldn't have, and now you're scrambling to apologize to your startled listener. The rest of the conversation is anything but relaxing for either of you.

Conversational boo-boos are common, and practically everyone makes one from time to time. Most blunders stem from a momentary lapse in judgment or a mistaken attempt at humor, but even accidental gaffes can cause you embarrassment and create tension between you and others. With a little practice and forethought, however, your words can work as you want them to: to bless others and build up your relationships.

When you are in a conversation, give it your complete attention. Focus on the person and on what he or she is saying. Avoid questionable jokes and impulsive comments, and resist the urge to jump right in when the other person comes to the end of a sentence. A momentary pause while you consider your response never diminishes a conversation. Rather, it deepens a friendship.

If someone tells an inappropriate joke or makes an offensive comment to you, graciously accept the person's apology. Let the matter drop immediately, and do your best to ease the person's embarrassment.

Admit You Need Answers

14

Your child asks you why there are bad people in the world. Your friend asks why God would allow her sister to die of cancer. This world is filled with questions, and trying to be the one with the answers is inviting stress to camp out indefinitely in your head.

As much as our logical brains want to deny it, some questions don't have answers, at least not answers we can understand and digest. Sometimes the ways of God, even the natural order of things and how God interacts with that part of his creation, are simply beyond us or at least not accessible to us. All we need to know is that God is handling what he has not asked us to handle.

The best response when someone asks you a question you can't answer is to tell the truth: "I don't know, but God does. There is so much more out there than our human minds can comprehend. We just must trust him." Then take your own advice.

*Known to God
from eternity are
all His works.*

Acts 15:18, NKJV

*Start a journal of unanswered questions. These should be
specific. Write them and commit them to God in prayer.
You may never know the answers, but you will be more
at peace knowing the answers are in his hands.*

15

Get Back to Basics

When did your life become so complicated? You think back, and it feels as if you're spinning. Days and weeks are flying by so quickly you can barely remember them. Where did all the good things go—quiet moments to spend with loved ones, and time to read, watch a movie, or just be alone with your thoughts?

We all reach a point in life when it's beneficial to stop to make adjustments. These are liberating moments, opportunities to eliminate those things that aren't working and reestablish boundaries and core values. It's like a lifestyle makeover, a return to the basics.

Genius is the ability to reduce the complicated to the simple.

C. W. Ceram

Think through your responsibilities with an eye for what you can hand over to someone else. Family obligations are nontransferable, of course. God expects you to take care of your family and to do so in a joyful, loving manner. You should hang on to your passions as well. They provide connections with the gifts and talents God has given you. Judge everything else by its relationship to inner peacefulness and calm.

Avoid sudden adjustments that leave others stranded. Instead, determine where change is needed, give plenty of notice, and allow someone else the opportunity to step up.

Soak in the Tub

16

Some time away from your stressful life would be good. You need a vacation, a break in the action. One answer might be to visit one of those pricey spa resorts and sign up for a massage or a mud bath. With fewer than five minutes of preparation, however, you can unwind in spa-like luxury right in your own bathtub.

Start by turning off your phone, turning on some soft music, and lighting a scented candle. Gather up a big, soft, clean bath towel; bath salts or bubble bath; a fragrant body lotion; and a tall glass of ice water. Draw a warm, deep bath, and climb in. You'll feel your neck and shoulders relax and your arms and legs lose their tension as you luxuriate in warmth, fragrance, and music. When you're ready to step out of your bath, slip into comfortable pajamas or a lounging robe.

This strategy works well regardless of gender, age, or social standing. You won't have to wait for an appointment, and you can't beat the price.

There is nothing like staying at home for real comfort.

Jane Austen

∽≫⊛≪∾

While you are relaxing your body, relax your mind as well by turning your thoughts to the warmth and purity of God's love for you. Consider how good it is to be able to relax because he has everything under control.

17

Do the Right Thing

A sticky situation is developing at work, and you find your-self right in the middle of it. Your coworker is stealing from the boss and urging you to do the same. He regales you with his flawed reasoning. It's a big company. No one will ever even notice. But your heart is telling you something else. You don't want any part of it. You are wise to hold your ground.

The ways of the LORD are right; the righteous walk in them.

Hosea 14:9, NIV

Going against your conscience is a loser's game. You may reap a few unearned benefits up front—some easy cash or perks—but sooner or later there is a price to pay, even if you are never caught with your hand in the cookie jar. Doing the right thing, on the other hand, pays off indefinitely with peace of mind, lack of guilt and inner turmoil, and no fear of your duplicity being revealed.

Doing the right thing is a winner's game. The small amount of stress you may encounter because of having to stand your ground is minuscule compared to the joy of living with clean hands and an unblemished heart.

Your conscience was given to you by God, and it is an amazing "right-o-meter." Learn to notice that subtle, unsettled feeling in the pit of your stomach that signals something amiss. Heed it, and peace returns.

Enjoy a Cup of Herbal Tea

18

It's been a stressful day, a hurried evening, and now it's bedtime and you're trying to get to sleep. Rather than counting sheep or reaching for a sleeping pill, take a walk to your kitchen. Reach for your favorite mug, boil some water, and add a measure of herbal tea. Not only will you enjoy its warm, aromatic charm, but when you return to bed, you'll fall asleep more easily.

Specially formulated herbal teas offer delicious blends of various healthful herbs and spices. Herbal teas are naturally caffeine-free, so they won't cause nervousness, irritability, or tension. Herbs and spices in herbal teas possess healing properties and give off exotic, relaxing fragrances. Many herbal teas are especially formulated for the reduction of stress and the promotion of sleep.

Long before the advent of the sleeping pill, God provided a natural and pleasant way to fall into the embrace of a good night's rest. Why count sheep any longer?

I lie down and sleep;
I wake again, for the
LORD sustains me.

Psalm 3:5, NRSV

Select an herbal tea with peppermint, spearmint, chamomile,
or ginseng as the primary herb. These herbs
are noted for promoting relaxation and sleep,
and they make a perfect bedtime beverage.

31

19

Become a Stargazer

I look at your heavens, the work of your fingers, the moon and the stars, which you have set in place.

Psalm 8:3, ESV

Step outside on a cool, clear night and look up into the night sky. Let yourself be captivated by the canopy of twinkling stars in God's vast universe. It's the world's best and oldest light show, guaranteed to give you perspective and allow you to rest in the shadow of God's greatness. If he made all this, you reason, surely he's mighty enough to help with any troubling circumstance in your life.

Anxiety and stress build within us when we begin to think ourselves solely responsible for what goes on here on earth. Gazing into the heavens is a wonderful way to remind ourselves that we are just part of the grand scheme of things. We are beloved, intelligent, caring, and yet wholly dependent on God and others. Stargazing keeps us humble, and humility keeps us from taking on more than we should.

When you feel the weight of the world on your shoulders, relax for a little while under the stars and soak up the greatness of God.

Find out when the next meteor shower is expected in your area. Plant your lawn chair or chaise longue as far from the streetlights as possible. Turn off most of the house lights, grab a flashlight, and prepare to be dazzled.

Don't Rely on Your Memory

20

Too late you realize that you have completely overlooked an important meeting at work or forgotten to send out letters for the neighborhood maintenance meeting. What's going on?

The most common reasons for forgetfulness are age, anxiety, anger, illness, fatigue, and, yes, that too-familiar monster, stress. The big S can drag you into a vicious cycle. Stress causes you to forget, and then the forgotten obligation creates more stress. Fortunately, there's no reason in this age of technology to rely solely on your memory.

It's possible to program even the most basic cell phone with alerts to remind you of appointments. Your phone can also store phone numbers and other critical information. If that doesn't work for you, keep an appointment book. Use it to remind you of business information as well as to pick up your children early from school and take the dog to the vet.

Give your tired, overtaxed, and stressed brain the assistance it needs. It's the right thing to do.

Memory [is] like a purse—if it be over-full that it cannot shut, all will drop out of it.

Thomas Fuller

❧

Explore all the applications your cell phone provides. Most will allow you to store names and other information you may have trouble recalling, especially when you're under pressure. Even if you don't need it, knowing you have access will help.

21

Find an Animal to Pet

*You care for
people and
animals alike,
O Lord.*

Psalm 36:6, NLT

The minute you walk in the door, you're greeted by the enthusiastic yips of your canine friend. You're smothered in affectionate nudges by your feline companion. No matter how stressful your day may have been, seeing your pet makes you feel better.

Animals touch your heart with their unabashed cuteness, uncomplicated personalities, and unconditional love. They also improve your health. As you watch a kitten chase her tail, or as you rub the chin of a grateful puppy, your blood pressure drops measurably. As you stroke an animal's soft coat, your muscles relax and your mood lifts. Even watching the rhythmic movements of fish in a tank or listening to the chirps of a parakeet provides you with physical relaxation, tension release, and emotional comfort.

Make the simple, cheerful, mood-enhancing presence of an animal part of your life. Enjoy its playful antics and free affection. An animal can help you get rid of stress the natural way—just by doing what God created it to do.

*If you cannot keep a pet in your home, volunteer to walk dogs
or play with cats at your local animal shelter. The joy you
provide the animal will be returned many times over.*

Watch What You Eat

22

After a long day at the office or ferrying kids from one activity to another, you come home and plop down on the sofa. Your nerves are jangled, and your stress level is over the top. Next thing you know, you're downing a bag of chips. You feel better for a little while, but not for long.

It's easy to turn to food when you are feeling the edginess of life. Traditional comfort foods—typically high-carbohydrate snacks—can alter your mood by inducing serotonin and dopamine synthesis in your brain. In the short run, they work wonders, leaving you calmer and less stressed. In the long run, however, those carbs should be coupled with proteins like tuna, cottage cheese, or a protein bar to bring a little balance.

There will be days when nothing takes the edge off like a salty, sugary snack. Go ahead and ease your pain. Just make sure you add a little protein. The body God gave you works best when it's in balance.

Use wisdom and understanding to establish your home; let good sense fill the rooms with priceless treasures.

Proverbs 24:3-4, CEV

Nuts are a satisfying yet healthy snack. One ounce of cashews, for example, adds about 170 calories, 7 grams of carbohydrates, 6 grams of protein, and 15 grams of fat—a great balanced combination. Low-fat yogurt is also a good choice.

35

23

Open Your Heart to Love

Beloved, let us love one another, because love is from God; everyone who loves is born of God and knows God.

1 John 4:7, NRSV

Maybe it was a romance that turned sour or a friendship that ended badly. Whatever the case, you've been burned by love and you now protect yourself by keeping others at arm's length. If this describes your situation, you're missing the best of God's gifts and blessings.

Forget about money and fame; the people in your life are what matter. They share your secrets, pick you up and brush you off when you fall on your face, and congratulate you when you do well. They believe in your dreams and inspire you to greatness. In the end, protecting yourself from the hurt of love only deprives you of the goodness and light love brings.

It could be that you've been holding back for a long time, with the pressure building inside. If so, it's time to relax and take a chance on love again. Let your heart open slowly, building a connection with one person and then another. One bright morning you'll wake up and realize you've learned to love again.

When you find yourself struggling with the decision to open yourself to someone, spend some time talking to God about him or her. If that person is part of God's plan, you will find stress and anxiety giving way to peace.

Give the Gift of Acceptance

24

Your best friend is a super gal, but you're certain she would look better if she changed her wardrobe. You decide to tell her. You love everything about your new boyfriend except for his taste in tunes, so you set out to change his musical diet. Perhaps you should think twice.

Changing others is rarely achievable, and even your best intentions may produce deep-seated stress in your relationships. Instead, make an effort to change the way you see others. By embracing people in your life as God's unique creations, you avoid the trap of focusing on their shortcomings. Only God is perfect; the rest of us grow in that direction at various speeds.

God knows everything there is to know about you, and he loves you anyway. He's aware of your flaws and celebrates your strengths. He looks for growth, but for now he accepts you just the way you are. That feels good, doesn't it? Follow his lead by giving those you love the gift of acceptance.

With compassion, we see benevolently our own human condition and the condition of our fellow beings. We drop prejudice. We withhold judgment.

Christina Baldwin

Before you try to change someone, ask yourself if you think God would agree with your assessment. Or would he say he loves that person just the way he or she is? This simple test can help you avoid stress and strain in your relationships.

Overcoming Perfectionism

Perfectionism and stress are inseparable. If nothing short of absolute perfection will suffice for any project you tackle, you invite stress from start to finish. While your commitment to high standards is admirable, you can trade the anxiety of perfectionism for the reward of excellence.

Perfectionism lures you into thinking you must perform flawlessly on every occasion. A project at home or church, in school, or in the workplace or community becomes not a welcome chance to participate, but a tense challenge to reach a perfect finish. Tension builds as you go, and finally, at the end, you feel more defeated than elated, more disappointed than pleased. No matter how many people praise your work, you're not happy because the project wasn't flawless.

Now think about the same project, only this time you aim for excellence. You know the project will be a challenge, but you welcome the opportunity to learn new skills and use your creativity. You're excited to see how well you can do. You enjoy the process, you give your best effort, and when it's finished, you step back and take stock. Sure, you could do a few things differently next time. Overall, however, the project has turned out well. You feel relaxed about yourself and your abilities, and you happily accept the compliments that come your way.

Keep in mind that only God is perfect and that pure perfection lies beyond human ability. Excellence, however, can be yours when you bring planning, pleasure, energy, and effort to everything you do.

Top Ten Things to Do

10. Examine your motives for desiring perfection.

9. Accept yourself and others as imperfect human beings.

8. Forgive yourself and others for mistakes.

7. Learn from your mistakes and failures.

6. Replace criticism with affirmation.

5. Set realistic, achievable goals.

4. Strive for excellence over perfection.

3. Take pleasure in the process.

2. Praise yourself for doing your best.

1. Ask God to help you strive for excellence.

25

Be Kind to a Stranger

Dangers are inherent in the world, and you find yourself avoiding strangers more and more, growing increasingly uncomfortable and cynical. As time goes by, you begin to feel the stress of living in what you consider a hostile environment.

Then one day you see a young mother trying to juggle two small children and a cart full of groceries. On an impulse, you ask if you can return her cart for her, leaving her free to get the kids buckled in and be on her way. It's a small gesture with a big payback. For the first time in a long time, you imagine that there are still good people in the world, people who offer kindness and people who gladly receive it.

Fear can cause isolation, stress, and depression. But kindness brings light, joy, and release. Open your eyes to see the people whom God has placed in your path. Reach out and soak up the light and life your caring gestures bring.

*Make it your business to commit at least one conscious act of
kindness each day. It won't abolish the negative influences in
the world, but it will help you keep your world balanced.*

Develop a Love for Literature 26

Some people think of literature as the classic novels that high school teachers assign the class to read. Others would say literature refers to complex tomes best left to graduate students and professors. If your definition falls into either of those categories, consider a fresh definition: literature is any book worthy of your time and attention.

True literature has the power to take you into different worlds, open you to new ideas, make you laugh, lift your spirits, and bring you the knowledge and wisdom of the ages. It has the capacity to inspire, guide, and instruct you. You can find literature in the form of a short story or a multivolume series, written a few millennia ago or only yesterday. The Bible, for example, was written thousands of years ago, and yet its message touches and changes lives today.

Read books worthy of your time and attention. Leave stress behind as you journey to faraway lands of mind, heart, and spirit.

Select a book that piques your interest, and forget about the "rule" that books started must be finished. There are no rules. Discover the joy and relaxation of reading for fun.

All Scripture is breathed out by God and profitable for teaching, for reproof, for correction, and for training in righteousness.

2 Timothy 3:16, ESV

27

Play with a Child

The dream vacation that you planned and saved for finally happened. You were sure you'd come back refreshed, free of stress, a new person. You did have a great time, but the rest and relaxation you expected didn't happen. Instead, you returned exhausted and frazzled to a pile of work that stacked up in your absence.

Children seem to have a different perspective on play than adults do. It seems effortless, doesn't it? They open their gifts on Christmas morning and then play with the boxes they came in. They find delight in simple actions like chasing butterflies and twirling in circles. Their play is effortless, renewable, and free from stress. Wouldn't it be nice to know what they know?

Join children at play, and you will quickly discover that their joy comes from simply interacting with what is right in front of them and unleashing their imagination, creativity, and laughter. They have no worries about money, logistics, or pressure-packed schedules. They simply have good, old-fashioned fun.

Jesus said, "Let the little children come to Me, and do not forbid them; for of such is the kingdom of heaven."

Matthew 19:14, NKJV

Invite a child to go with you to the park or playground, and allow the child to choose the activities. Then loosen up and play along. At the end of your time together, you'll both be thinking it was a great day.

Make Duplicate Keys

28

The clock is ticking, and you're running late to work. Finally, when the door is open and you're ready to roll, you discover that you don't have your car keys. You frantically search every room and every jacket and pants pocket— nothing. You dump out your purse and search through the contents for the third time—nothing. By this time, your stress level is off the charts.

Door keys, car keys, office keys, locker keys, all those keys you depend on every day can easily hide under sofa cushions, in the lining of last season's handbag, beneath piles of laundry, in too many places to count. But a little advance planning can save you.

Rather than tell yourself you'll put those keys back where they belong next time, have duplicate keys made for all your locks. Keep duplicates on a separate key chain in a secure yet accessible place. That way if you lose a key, you can use the spare and engage in search-and-recover at a more convenient time.

When you're stuck in a spiral, to change all aspects of the spin you need only to change one thing.

Christina Baldwin

Keep keys to the front and back doors of your home on separate key chains. For all your keys, choose large, sturdy key chains so you can easily find your keys if you drop or misplace them.

29

Take Care of Important Papers

The car you've been looking for is finally about to be yours. But before the dealer will take your trade-in, you have to produce the title. You rush home to get it, but it seems to be hiding. You look for two hours with no success. It's maddening.

The Bible offers wisdom concerning these types of routine stressors. The Bible urges an attitude of preparedness. And you might be surprised how little effort it takes to be prepared. Choose one place in your home where you will keep your important documents—insurance policies, birth certificates, Social Security cards, passports, car and house titles, medical records, wills, and important contact information your family might need in the event of an emergency.

Once you have all your documents together, make copies. Keep the copies in a safe place in your home, in a filing cabinet, or on a flash drive, and tell a family member or close friend where they can be found. Put the originals in a safety-deposit box at your bank or in some other secure location. You'll wonder why you didn't do it sooner.

Ants—they aren't strong, but they store up food all summer.

Proverbs 30:25, NLT

Purchase a fireproof, waterproof box or cabinet for your home in which to keep your copied documents. An actual safe isn't needed, just something to protect your copies in the event of a fire or flood.

Allow Yourself to Ask for Help

30

Your best friend tells you she needs your help. Immediately, you ask what you can do, and you're happy to give her the assistance she needs. Yet when you find yourself in need, you say nothing to anyone.

Whether this is in response to a strong sense of independence or even a reluctance to burden other people with your problems, it creates a stress that God never intended. None of us walk in this world alone. We need each other. After all, God only occasionally chooses to fix our troubled situations supernaturally. Rather, he equips and sends us to act on behalf of one another.

When you reject the help of others—even if it is simply by omission—you deny them the opportunity to do God's work and receive the blessing that goes along with it. So when your stress level reaches a high pitch and your burdens seem like they are going to overwhelm you, reach out and let those who love you know what you need.

Bear one another's burdens, and so fulfill the law of Christ.

Galatians 6:2, ESV

Make a list of people you can depend on for help in various situations, and include their contact information. The next time you need help, encouragement, or someone to listen, pick up your list and call.

31

Invest in Flowers

I do not think I have ever seen anything more beautiful than the bluebell I have been looking at. I know the beauty of our Lord by it.

Gerard Manley Hopkins

Entering a room, you see only what needs doing. There are beds to make, rugs to vacuum, and shelves to dust. A desk is covered with work, and the next project is waiting to be planned. Before you've even made a move to start the first task, you feel stressed out.

Then your eyes rest on a vase of bright flowers that seem like an oasis for your spirit. You pause a moment to drink in the playful smile of a daisy and admire the simple elegance of a lily. You touch the velvety petal of a rose and bend to savor its sweet perfume. You linger a moment more to take in God's handiwork and thank him for the renewal and refreshment a simple flower offers to all who take the time to look.

A vase of flowers may not make the beds or get that new project up and running, but it's bound to make you feel happier and more relaxed as you go about your day.

Most people think of fresh flowers as too pricey for everyday enjoyment, but many stores carry fresh flower bouquets for less than five or ten dollars. And the flowers can last at least a week and maybe two. It's a small price to pay for the therapy they bring.

Eat a Meal by Candlelight

32

A table carefully set for dinner. The aroma of herbs and spices coming from the kitchen. The flickering warmth of a candle. Is this a special occasion? Is there something to celebrate? Maybe, but maybe not. Maybe it's only an ordinary meal on an ordinary day. Maybe it's for a family of four, just the two of you, or simply for you.

Routine days and routine meals run together, and the goodness and pleasure of food get lost in the rush to eat and get to the next place you need to be. Yet when you think about it, you realize your food is a blessing from God, a blessing to be savored and appreciated. Good food eaten with gratitude and attentiveness not only keeps you healthy, but it also relaxes you and renews your body and spirit.

At your next meal, let the soft glow of a lighted candle remind you to be thankful for the gift of food and for the comfort, relaxation, and pleasure it brings.

The eyes of all look expectantly to You, and You give them their food in due season.

Psalm 145:15, NKJV

Make your next meal special by inviting a friend or two to join you. Fix something simple like spaghetti with marinara sauce or macaroni and cheese. Ask one friend to bring a salad, the other, bread. Light a candle, and spend an evening relaxing over food and good conversation.

47

33

Abandon Perfectionism

People praise what you do, but their words bring little satisfaction. Instead, you dwell on the minor goof, the trivial slipup, the tiny flaw. You do everything with excellence, but you want nothing short of perfection.

If you're a perfectionist, you're familiar with the stress and anxiety you bring to everything you do. From your daily responsibilities to your chosen hobbies, your critical eye quickly glosses over what's right and singles out what's wrong. Sadly, no process is a pleasure and no finish a celebration.

The skies will brighten when you can accept one important premise: God alone is perfect. For the rest of us, perfection is not achievable this side of heaven. Embrace yourself as an imperfect human being. Don't worry; this won't turn you into a slacker. It's simply a way to better understand yourself. Once you can accept the flaws, you will be free to celebrate the fabulous in what you do and appreciate the gifts and talents God has placed in you.

Striving for excellence motivates you; striving for perfection is demoralizing.

Harriet Braiker

At the completion of a task or project, list side by side the excellent aspects of what you've done and the things you were not happy with. You'll quickly note that the cheers heavily outweigh the boos.

Keep a Journal

34

You're a busy person and have many responsibilities to family and work, and that's just the beginning. Somehow you get it all done, but there is little time left to appreciate blessings, exercise creativity, or evaluate your true feelings. You live with unresolved stress. If you are nodding yes right now, you might want to consider keeping a personal journal.

A journal is a place for you to record your private thoughts and meditations. It gives voice to excellent ideas and insightful observations you might not have realized you had. It lets you express yourself without worrying what others may think and gives you a means to work out productive solutions to complex problems. In an organized way, your journal allows you to note the events of your days and become more aware of God's plans and purpose for your life.

Daily journaling need not be time-consuming or cumbersome. A few minutes each day spent with your journal will find you better able to cope with your anxieties and more in touch with your best self.

Do not let loyalty and faithfulness forsake you; bind them around your neck, write them on the tablet of your heart.

Proverbs 3:3, NRSV

Choose one of the many kinds of journals available, from a simple spiral-bound notebook to a decorative hardcover book with inspirational quotations or daily thought-starters. Write as much or as little as you like.

49

35

Change Your Diet

Vegetables are the food of the earth; fruit seems more the food of the heavens.

Sepal Felicivant

With a few additions and subtractions through the years, you eat what you've always eaten. Food always makes you feel better, more calm and less stressed-out. But now you are sitting in the doctor's office listening to a discussion of your weight problem or diet-related health concern like diabetes or high cholesterol. You feel that your old friend, food, has turned on you. Your anxiety triples.

Consider this: food is not the culprit. The problem lies in what foods you choose and how you prepare them. Rather than focus on what you're giving up, think about what you are adding. Trying new things and learning new cooking techniques can be fun and relaxing.

Try substituting one food for another each week—whole-grain bread for white bread, for example, or a plant-based margarine for butter. Try some of your favorite recipes grilled or baked rather than fried. Food is still your friend, a bona fide gift from God, in fact. You just have to change the outfit it's been wearing.

Pay a visit to a natural-foods store and spend some time checking things out. In the produce section alone, you will likely see fruits and vegetables you aren't familiar with. Buy a small amount of a few and try them out at home.

Discover Your Passion

36

The neighbor pruning her roses, your uncle varnishing a tabletop in the garage, a concert pianist performing with an enraptured expression. You've seen it in their faces, haven't you? These people know what they love and have found a place where they can be fully relaxed, lost in the joy of it.

It's possible that you have never given yourself permission to explore the world of pastimes outside the boundaries of your daily responsibilities. But you can be sure that God has placed something special inside you, something worth searching for, something that can breathe new life into your soul.

Ask yourself: Is there an undeveloped talent you would like to pursue? What sports, activities, or cultural arts draw you in, fascinate you, or capture your attention? Follow your instincts, and they will tell you what you need to know. Find your passion, and you will always have a lifeboat to jump into when the storms of life threaten to sink your ship.

Whatever you do, do it heartily, as to the Lord and not to men.

Colossians 3:23, NKJV

The local community college offers classes in everything from self-defense to jewelry making. These are usually short-term and inexpensive, providing an interesting way to have fun and do some passion hunting.

Reaching Out to Others

If you're like most people, a roomful of strangers is a frightening place.
You feel uneasy until someone walks up to you and welcomes you into
the group. Then, your tension disappears. You relax and enjoy yourself.
What's more, the person who has welcomed you feels good, too.

You can overcome the natural stress of stepping outside familiar surroundings by focusing not on your fears but on other people. Smile and make eye contact. When someone responds to your friendly approach, introduce yourself and make a few brief comments. Your actions will put you at ease, and they will put the other person at ease, too—a person who may have wanted to reach out to you but wasn't brave enough to do so.

Interestingly, the key to stress management is said to be about taking charge, feeling empowered about your schedule, environment, thoughts, and emotions. Taking the initiative in social gatherings provides a simple opportunity with an almost immediate payday. When you receive a positive response, your confidence rises and you feel more at ease.

It's also true that God created us to be social beings. Simply put, we need one another and flourish in the sunshine of positive human relationships. Each time we make a connection, however brief, we feel affirmed and less isolated.

The next time you find yourself in a roomful of strangers, choose a likely suspect, extend your hand with a smile, and get ready to make a new friend.

Top Ten Things to Do

10. Refuse to accept social stereotypes.

9. Never judge based on appearance.

8. Risk speaking to strangers.

7. Put others in the best possible light.

6. Challenge unfair discriminatory practices.

5. Minimize differences and maximize similarities.

4. Defend individuals and groups that are vilified without cause.

3. Speak kindly of others, in keeping with the truth.

2. Recognize everyone as a child of God.

1. Treat others the way you would like them to treat you.

37

Get Lots of Sunshine

After only a few gray days, you're longing to see the sun again. When at last the clouds part and a few soft rays pour through your windowpane, you take notice. You smile, breathe deeply, and welcome God's gift of light and warmth back into your life.

Sunshine is essential to your health and well-being. From the sun's rays, your body absorbs vitamin D, which is known to strengthen the immune system and protect the body from various diseases. Sunshine also acts as a mood enhancer, and the happier you feel, the more relaxed you feel. God, in his goodness, offers the best health and mood booster to anyone who steps outside or sits by a window.

Even a few minutes of natural light each day will energize your body and lift your spirits. On every sunshiny day, take five or ten minutes to catch the rays and give thanks to God for the warmth and the moments of relaxation he has so richly provided.

A day without sunshine is like, you know, night.

Steve Martin

If your location or circumstances limit your exposure to sunlight, you can get a similar benefit by eating vitamin D–rich foods like cold-water fish, egg yolks, and butter or by taking a vitamin D supplement each day.

Live in the Moment

38

If you're like most people, you tend to live in the past and in the future. You mull over what happened yesterday— what you could have said, what you should have done—and you're worried about what could happen tomorrow. No wonder you're stressed out today.

God can ease your anxiety about your past shortcomings. With the promise of his presence, God removes your fear of the unknown as you look forward to the future. With his promises in your heart, you're able to live fully, trustingly, and joyfully in the present moment. You're open to today's beauty and miracles, its opportunities and challenges. You're living the way God intends—in the day, the hour, the moment he has given.

Refuse to spend time today dwelling on negative, stress-producing, and unproductive thoughts about the past and future. Instead, focus on what you're doing right now and take delight in the blessing of this moment in time.

The living moment
is everything.

D. H. Lawrence

Clear your mind of all distractions and focus on the
present moment. Be attentive to all your senses—
what you see, hear, smell, touch, and taste.
Praise God for the miracle of this moment.

39

Get Up Fifteen Minutes Early

I have to hurry. If this is your first thought in the morning, your day is off to a stressful start. You almost certainly will feel rushed all day and frustrated by how little you actually accomplish. God's best for you doesn't include your being defeated before you begin.

A simple way to resolve the problem of a rushed, stressful morning is to take control of your routine. First, prepare the night before by laying out clothes, fixing lunches, and organizing the needs of the next day. Second, make sure you go to bed early enough to get a full night's rest. And third, set the alarm a little earlier than you have in the past.

Just a fifteen-minute head start can make a significant difference and provide a little extra time to accommodate unexpected delays. You have plenty of those, right? Soon you'll discover how calm, pleasant, and unhurried your day can be with those extra minutes in the morning.

Each morning you listen to my prayer, as I bring my requests to you and wait for your reply.

Psalm 5:3, CEV

Keep those extra few minutes in the morning for yourself. Use them to get dressed in peace or to gather your thoughts before the rest of the family is awake and things get hectic. You'll come to love those first few minutes in your day.

Stop Negative Thoughts

40

The hard work is behind you, and now it's time for your big presentation. You should be confident and self-assured. Instead, your thoughts are beating up on you. Every negative "what-if" is swimming around in your head, and by the time you stand up and face your colleagues, you are one big ball of stress.

That never has to happen to you again. Your mind, like every other part of your body, is ultimately under your control. You don't have to be held hostage by your mental default mode. You can override it. The Bible teaches that human beings have been given the power to change not only their behavior but also their thoughts.

When negative thoughts begin to assail you, you have the authority to shoo them away, and you have the power to choose to think about good things instead. You may have to bully your thoughts into submission, but they will eventually comply if you stand your ground. Your stress will melt away like snow on a warm and sunny hillside.

If there is any excellence, if there is anything worthy of praise, think about these things.

Philippians 4:8, ESV

Learn to differentiate between negative thoughts and realistic thoughts. Negative thoughts are self-destructive and unproductive. Realistic thoughts are designed to alert you to a problem like physical illness or danger ahead.

41

Live Moderately

*Do yourself a favor
by having good
sense—you will
be glad you did.*

Proverbs 19:8, CEV

When it's too much, you know it. You feel anxiety if you spend too much, and you feel drained if you do too much. Eating or drinking too much brings health problems, and working or playing too much throws life out of balance. Too much is too much.

God desires for you to find pleasure in the resources you rightfully possess. Apply your talents, follow your passions, and take advantage of your opportunities. God gave them to you to use, both for yourself and on behalf of others. When any one thing becomes an obsession, an addiction, or an overwhelming desire, however, it takes the control out of your hands and causes you to feel conflicted. That inner conflict is the enemy of peace and calm. If left unchecked, stress can build to the breaking point.

Delight in the good things God has given to you, but possess and use them as he intended—in moderation.

*Your body will tell you where your boundaries
should be if you are listening. It's like a little tug
inside, an unsettled feeling in your gut that triggers
a distress signal to your brain. When you feel the tug,
acknowledge it and honor your boundaries.*

Find an Enjoyable Exercise 42

It's early afternoon, and you can already feel tension building in a few problem spots like your neck, shoulders, back, and legs. You might reach for a bottle of pain reliever or just try to ignore it. What you probably wouldn't do is think about getting some exercise.

Exercise provides an opportunity for you to release the tension that's been building up and for your body to relax. In addition, the extra oxygen that exercise draws into your bloodstream refreshes your mind. That's how God intended your body to work. Even if you have limited mobility, your lungs, heart, muscles, and bones could benefit from exercise.

How you get that exercise is completely up to you. Some people love to go to the gym. But you may not be comfortable with the cost or the commitment of time that requires. An option might be to take a walk at lunchtime. Ask a friend or a coworker to go along. You might also purchase a video that teaches simple stretching exercises. Your body will thank you.

Most people choose an exercise technique based on what they believe will be most effective. Avoid that pitfall. Instead, go with what you think would be fun. If it's not fun, you'll soon tire of it, and exercise will become a stressful chore.

Great things are not done by impulse, but by a series of small things brought together.

Vincent van Gogh

59

43

Draw, Color, Doodle

Do you remember how, as a young child, you could pick up a crayon and a sheet of paper and doodle? It was fun to explore color for color's sake, and you enjoyed the wonderful sensation of setting your imagination free in an uninhibited, visual form.

Though you probably consider it child's play, you might be surprised at how relaxing doodling can still be. Of course, there are a few rules, and the first one is "forget the rules." Release yourself from the obligation to color within the lines. Draw something as you think it should be drawn. That's, after all, the whole point. Life has too many rules, and much of your stress comes from working to comply. Becoming a self-professed artist gives you an opportunity to do something that need suit no one but yourself. It's liberating.

If drawing or coloring doesn't do it for you, try calligraphy or whatever suits your fancy. Let your imagination show you how to be a child again.

Visit a discount or big-box store to shop for inexpensive art supplies. Grab some art paper, colored pencils, crayons, markers, blue and black ink pens (not ballpoints), and a coloring book. Keep them in a basket near your favorite lounging spot.

Start on Your Taxes in January   *44*

April 15 is almost here, and you still don't have your taxes done. You've been rushing around looking for misplaced documents and receipts, and dreading that long line at the post office every April 14. No wonder you're stressed out.

Do yourself a favor this year and avoid the April crunch. The forms you need—1099s and W-2s—are required by law to be sent to you no later than February 15. While you're waiting for them to arrive, send for or print out any forms you will need and gather the previous year's receipts. As tax documents arrive in the mail, put them into a basket or small box reserved for tax-related material only. Then, in February, you're ready for the business of figuring your taxes or taking your documents to your tax preparer. By March, the job's complete.

Paying income taxes is something few people enjoy, unless, of course, you have a big refund coming. Get your tax return out of the way early so you can spend April 14 thanking God for your income.

*Jesus told them,
"Give the Emperor
what belongs to him
and give God what
belongs to God."*

Mark 12:17, CEV

*On January 1, place a basket on or near your desk specifically
for tax-related receipts. Make a habit of dropping all your
receipts in the basket throughout the year. When tax-
preparation time comes around, they'll be readily available.*

45

Cultivate Support

You've decided to accept a volunteer position in your community or take a course at the local university. You mention it to your family members and friends in passing, and they all seem agreeable. But when the realities of those extra time-consuming responsibilities come to bear, everyone seems surprised, and resentments—both yours and theirs—begin to build.

Live in harmony with each other.

Romans 12:16, NLT

Stress within the family unit is taxing and should be avoided. That's why it's so important to sit down with family members and discuss your new venture. Let them know, for example, "I'll be gone on Monday, Tuesday, and Thursday evenings for the next three months," or "I want you to know I'll be unreachable on Saturdays for the next three weeks." Explain your reasons for taking on this new project, and let them ask questions.

Your home and those in it are God's gift to you. Stop stress at the door by enlisting the support of those closest to you.

Keep a calendar on the refrigerator or somewhere else in the kitchen. Note the times you will be away or involved with study or preparation. Ask your family members to add their activities to the calendar as well.

Take Your Vitamins

46

Every night you fall into bed exhausted. You feel as if you're always fighting off a cold or some unnamed malady that saps your strength and makes everything more difficult. If you find yourself in this dilemma, you may need to make some serious lifestyle changes, but then again, it might be as simple as giving your body what it needs to recharge itself.

God's perfect plan, it would seem, is that your body receive what it needs for optimal function through the food you eat. Unfortunately, there are many reasons why you can no longer count on getting what you need from food alone. By all means eat right, but make sure you fill in the gaps in the nutrients your food offers by taking daily supplements of energy-rich, immunity-building, stress-relieving vitamins and minerals.

Why struggle just to get by? Make sure your body is well maintained and able to take on whatever your daily activities throw at it.

I will praise You, for I am fearfully and wonderfully made.

Psalm 139:14, NKJV

Make an appointment with your doctor to help you determine the vitamins you need each day given your diet, age, and overall health. Your doctor will also be able to tell you what supplements might interact negatively with any prescription medications you take.

47   Cut Back on the Media Crush

Lord, what do I look for? My hope is in you.

Psalm 39:7, NIV

Sit down in your favorite chair, grab the remote, and turn on the evening news. Just like that, you find yourself immersed in the world's worst woes. Violence, war, financial crashes, weather anomalies, corruption, murder, and mayhem all come at you from around the world at a heart-pounding pace. The life you lead is stressful enough without taking on far-flung conflicts, most of which you have no power to change in any way.

The truth is that a half hour of national news and a half hour of local news are more than adequate. Better yet, turn off the television and read the newspaper, a medium that is kinder and gentler on the senses.

Discard the media hype that you have an obligation to be fully informed concerning every issue. God didn't design your body to carry the weight of the world on your shoulders. View only what is essential, and pray about those issues that concern you.

❧

Choose one news item per day and pray about it. In a notebook or your journal, write down a one-line description of the situation and the date you prayed. Thank God for doing what you cannot.

Meditate on God and His Word

It's an awful feeling. Your feathers are ruffled, and you're agitated and unsettled. You try watching TV but find that it just makes things worse—too much violence and bad news. You try talking to a friend but soon realize you're only adding your friend's agitation to your own. Then you see a Bible lying on your desk. You pick it up and begin to read. You might not say it's a miracle, but soon you are feeling better.

If you view the Bible as little more than a holy book of instruction in an ancient religion, rethink that view. The Bible is much more than that. In actuality, it is a letter from God to humankind. Within its pages, he lays out the history of creation, his purposes and promises, and how we can enter into relationship with him, as well as nuggets of wisdom concerning how best to live.

Who better to advise you on relieving stress and relaxing in your circumstances than the one who created you in the first place?

These are written so that you will put your faith in Jesus as the Messiah and the Son of God. If you have faith in him, you will have true life.

John 20:31, CEV

Open your Bible to the book of Psalms and begin reading slowly. Stop when you come to a passage that grabs your attention. That verse may have been written thousands of years before you were born, but today it may be a personal note from God just for you.

Positive Thinking

What goes on in your head affects your overall well-being. When your mind buzzes with anxious, fearful, and fretful thoughts, your body responds with stress headaches, tense muscles, and unmanageable emotions. Learn to take charge of your thoughts, and you will gain peace of mind, body, and spirit.

Everyone has negative thoughts from time to time. They are simply the price we pay for living in an imperfect world. In fact, many of these negative thoughts are designed to make us aware of potential danger. When negative thoughts dominate your mind, however, they serve only to distort reality and weigh you down with overwhelming stress.

Just as you may choose who enters your home, you have the power to choose the thoughts you entertain in your mind. Be attentive to the kinds of thoughts you let in, especially when you're in a stressful situation. Ask: Do these thoughts reflect the whole truth of the matter, or only a small part? Are they beneficial to me and worth considering further? Will they lead to a constructive solution to the problem in front of me?

Open your heart and mind to God's presence in your life. Remember how things have worked out for the best in the past, and think about the blessings you have in your life right now. Allow room for a fresh perspective and productive, creative ideas to enter. Relax in God's protective embrace, and cultivate the company of positive thoughts and feelings.

Top Ten Things to Do

10. Banish negative and disparaging self-talk.

9. Cultivate a positive attitude and optimistic outlook.

8. Think and speak in positive, constructive terms.

7. Avoid negative people as much as possible.

6. Gather the facts rather than react to fear.

5. Get daily exercise, good nutrition, and adequate rest.

4. Learn to laugh and find the humor in your day.

3. Visualize yourself succeeding at the tasks in front of you.

2. Count your blessings, your successes, and your joys.

1. Praise God for his presence in your life.

49

Avoid Hot-Button Topics

In conversation avoid the extremes of forwardness and reserve.

John Byrom

When you enter the room, it is buzzing with casual conversation. Everyone seems to be having a good time until someone brings up a controversial subject and begins to expound. Suddenly the mood changes, and everyone shifts nervously from one foot to the other. While the topic may be highly relevant and all over the media, it may be the wrong place and the wrong time to discuss it.

Save unnecessary angst by refusing to be caught up in discussions better suited for small groups of trusted friends and family. Subjects such as religion and politics, for example, are usually emotion packed and stress inducing.

Honestly, just because some other person feels the need to challenge others with his or her thoughts and opinions does not mean you, or anyone else for that matter, should feel compelled to present a counter opinion. Silence does not necessarily mean agreement. In such situations, it's a good practice to stay calm, use your most gracious words, and with a congenial nod, simply walk away.

Before joining others in a business meeting or social gathering, think about the people you are likely to meet. Try to greet each person with a warm and positive statement or compliment. Meet inappropriate statements with a smile and a quick getaway.

Be Willing to Compromise 50

Do you find yourself at an impasse with your child, your coworker, your neighbor, or your spouse? You can feel your face reddening and your blood pressure rising, and you're getting nowhere. Maybe it's time for a little compromise.

Compromise often gets a bad rap as a diluter of truth and moral correctness. In reality, it is a tool more for good than for bad. It can better be described as an effective way to disarm disputes and bring peace and understanding to a situation. Compromise can actually strengthen rather than dilute, and it can emphasize points of truth and areas of agreement that have been muddled by trivialities.

The next time you find yourself in a high-anxiety face-off with someone, pause, take a breath, and give yourself a moment to consider what you might be willing to concede in order to resolve the situation. Offer what you can, and ask what the other person might be willing to offer in return.

God blesses those who work for peace, for they will be called the children of God.

Matthew 5:9, NLT

If there is a particularly difficult person in your life with whom you often disagree, list the areas where conflict most often occurs—a teenager's curfew, for example. Think about a possible compromise before you find yourself embroiled in a heated encounter.

51

Reframe Problems

Tough times never last, but tough people do.

Robert Schuller

A problem is floating around in your head, and you haven't been able to work out what to do about it. The more you think about it, the more clueless and stressed out you become. You may need to look at the problem with new eyes.

Viewed as negatives, problems are seen as obstacles, but viewed as potentially positive, problem solving can provide a creative challenge, a brainteasing opportunity, or even fun. For example, spring rains have left your backyard a mess. You aren't sure you have the time or the motivation to clean it all up. Flip to the positive, and you are asking how you can take advantage of the soft soil to make the backyard more usable and fun for family activities, gardening, or entertaining in the summer months. The problem has shifted from drudgery to promising new opportunities.

Begin by thanking God for the problem and asking him to help you look past the dark clouds and see the sunshine on the other side.

Take that problem that's been niggling at your brain and write it down. This strips the problem of its emotion and gives it the feel of a puzzle to be solved. You will then be better able to consider all the angles and apply logic and creativity to it.

Decide to Forgive

52

Someone has done you wrong, and you feel anger, frustration, and hurt welling up inside. You find yourself swallowing hard and taking deep breaths, and you're aware of a growing knot in the pit of your stomach. What can you do? Wait for an apology from the person who hurt you? What if an apology never comes?

Regardless of what the other person does, you can move on, shake off the stress, and resolve the situation in your own heart and mind by making the decision to forgive. Think of it this way: If you burn your finger, you rush to soak it in cold water. Immersing your finger in cold water ensures that the heat in the burn will be quenched and no further harm can be done. In much the same way, immersing your emotional hurt in forgiveness eliminates its power to keep doing damage.

You can't make choices for someone else, but you can certainly make them for yourself. Let God help you soak those offenses in forgiveness and relax in his goodness and mercy.

*Forgive anyone
who does you wrong,
just as Christ has
forgiven you.*

Colossians 3:13, CEV

It might not be appropriate or productive to voice your forgiveness to the person who offended you. Make it an inner work. Later, if the person asks for your forgiveness, you can say it's already been given.

71

53

Share Your Feelings

Some days you feel as if you're going to explode. The pressure inside keeps building, and you go through the day pushing it down, holding it back, afraid you will completely lose it.

Perhaps this is why the Bible says not to let the sun go down on your anger. In principle, this could apply to your feelings of sadness, regret, and fear as well. Letting off steam at the end of each day by sharing your feelings provides a safe outlet for the release of unhealthy pressure and stress. You may or may not have someone in your life you can share your feelings with on a regular basis, but whatever the case, God is always there, ready to listen, ready to comfort and counsel.

Take your issues to God at the end of each long day. Simply tell him what is on your mind. He won't judge, and he won't scold. He will listen, and he will help you find solutions over time. Trust him, and your sleep will be sweet.

If you have trouble verbalizing your feelings, keep
a journal next to your bed. Each night write out
your thoughts and feelings truthfully and in as much
detail as you are comfortable with. God won't be
shocked. He sees your heart anyway.

Keep the Big Picture in Mind

54

It's time to make a presentation at work, and you're feeling the nerves. The usual questions are jumping around in your brain: *What if I blow it, lose my place, come across looking really dumb? What if my coworker doesn't come through with the data I need to make my pitch? What if . . . ?*

Trying to relax in a situation like this is daunting, primarily because you are narrowly focused on one specific goal. Remind yourself of what you already know. One presentation does not a career make. Your life is not defined by one day, one situation, one success, or one failure. Not all your chips are riding on one outcome. Looking beyond the moment to the greater scheme of things will help you keep things in perspective.

God has a wonderful plan for your life. Relax and forget about the what-ifs.

When you find yourself stressed, ask yourself one question: Will this matter five years from now?

Catherine Pulsifer

When you find yourself struggling in a narrowly focused situation of any kind, take a moment to put your circumstance in context. Remind yourself that your life is big enough to absorb both the good and the bad one day can offer.

55 Relinquish Control

Sitting in a long line of traffic, you honk your horn. Or you're locked in a futile attempt to convince a friend to do the right thing. These are understandable but frustrating situations. A great many issues in life are under your control, but a great many are not. Knowing the difference will save you stress and wasted effort.

I prayed to the LORD, and he answered me. He freed me from all my fears.

Psalm 34:4, NLT

Ultimately, you can't control how people drive, what people wear, or how people will vote in the next election. You can't control the elements, the economy, or the disposition of foreign wars. What you can do is put your life in God's hands and ask him to help you sort the cans from the can'ts. There is peace in knowing someone bigger than yourself is in charge, someone who sees all and has the power to do what you cannot.

Would you really want to be in control of everything in this world? That's a very big job, and it could be pretty stressful.

The need to control things around you is typically the result of fear. When you find yourself wanting to control a situation, stop and ask yourself what you are afraid will happen. Then ask for God's help to overcome that fear.

Adjust Your Expectations

56

Have you ever launched enthusiastically into a project, only to realize at some point that you had bitten off more than you could chew? Maybe it was a landscaping project. You looked around and imagined a koi pond in one corner, roses in the other. You saw a new tree surrounded by a lush lawn. You eagerly invested in what you needed, but soon the project began to feel weighty. You heard yourself praying, "O Lord, what have I gotten myself into?"

This has happened to almost everyone at one time or another. It might not have been the lawn. Maybe it was a dinner party or a remodeling project. You just didn't think it through, and your expectations were out of line.

All unrealistic expectations produce stress. Carefully plan and pray about projects like tearing out the kitchen or inviting your children to move back in. It isn't possible to anticipate every variable, but you will at least have an opportunity to weigh the pros and cons.

We make our own plans, but the LORD *decides where we will go.*

Proverbs 16:9, CEV

***

Before deciding on a big project, sit down, pray about it, and create a plan on paper. Estimate the cost, time frame, labor, possible obstacles, helpful resources, and so forth. Keep the plan where you can refer to it often.

57

Choose to Stop Struggling

Onward and upward. Those words have described your attitude for years, but now they're losing appeal. You're in a constant state of tension because you keep pushing yourself to the next level, looking ahead to see where you can go next, maneuvering to the head of the line. And when someone else claims the prize, you have the added stress of disappointment and self-reproach.

He brought me out into a spacious place.

Psalm 18:19, NIV

If the struggle to reach onward and upward isn't doing it for you anymore, consider trading it for the peace of branching outward. Imagine how it would feel to use your talents to the fullest not because you're angling for something better, but because you're happy right where you are.

It takes confidence in yourself and knowledge of your true gifts to choose something other than a frantic struggle to get to the top. Some might call it settling, but the Bible calls it recognizing the good, bountiful, and spacious place God has put you in right now.

Write a short paragraph on what genuine success would look like to you given your desires, drive, and circumstances. Would you be happier, less stressed, and more satisfied branching outward instead of struggling upward?

Really Listen to Others

58

It's only 9:00 a.m. and one of your coworkers has already said something that set you off. Now you're steaming. Once you calm down, you ask her to clarify her remarks. That's when you realize she wasn't saying what you thought she was saying at all. You just weren't listening.

Misunderstandings can disrupt your day, waste your time, and keep you agitated and stressed. And they are so unnecessary. Think about it this way: Our world is made up of billions of unique individuals, all with varying thought patterns and personal circumstances. Add to that widely differing meanings for common words, and communication problems are bound to happen.

It probably isn't practical to think you can avoid all misunderstandings, but you can certainly do a lot to alleviate them by simply paying attention, being fully engaged when someone is speaking to you, and keeping statements in context. Getting it right the first time is so much better than having to double back and go through it again.

Be quick to listen, slow to speak, and slow to get angry.

James 1:19, NLT

In every conversation, remember to SUF (seek understanding first). Before getting angry, repeat back what you heard the person say and ask if that is correct. If it is, then try to gain understanding by asking clarifying questions.

59

Get Enough Sleep

It is in vain that you rise up early and go late to rest, eating the bread of anxious toil; for he gives sleep to his beloved.

Psalm 127:2, NRSV

The stress from your day is causing you to lose sleep at night, and losing sleep at night is adding to the stress in your day. It's a vicious cycle and mighty frustrating. You fall into bed at night bone tired, then toss and turn for a couple of hours, unable to shut off your racing mind and get your body into a comfortable sleep position.

You can't afford to ignore this problem. Sleep is just too important. Sleep helps you be calm, alert, focused, less likely to fall or be involved in an accident, and more productive. Sleep helps maintain a solid immune system and a sharp memory, provides a way to work out solutions to problems, rejuvenates your cells, and strengthens your muscles and tissue.

In God's economy, human beings need to spend about one-third of each twenty-four-hour period sleeping. When you lie down at night, ask God to bless your mind and body with sleep. You'll be a better person for it.

When you miss sleep, your body incurs what is called a sleep deficit. It's essential to your body's health to make up that deficit and not let it become a habit to make do on short rations. If you've lost sleep, schedule a "sleep vacation": several days when you sleep undisturbed until you awaken spontaneously.

Let Someone Else Save the Planet

60

Someone is burning off the rain forest. The hole in the ozone is getting bigger. The ice floes are shrinking. The air, soil, lakes, and rivers are becoming more polluted by the day. Somebody has to do something. You lie awake at night thinking about it, trying to reason away the anxiety to no avail.

Feeling a sense of responsibility for the beautiful planet God placed us on is a good thing. But it's clear that God intended the care of the planet to be a unified effort. No one person can do it all. Rather than lying awake all night feeling anxious and guilty, find out what you can do to make a difference, and leave the rest to others. That might mean something as simple as organizing a neighborhood recycling drive or as difficult as lending your efforts to political lobbying or spending time in a small village somewhere in the world establishing a clean water supply.

The needs are incredibly great, but you can do only your part. Find out where you can make a difference, and trust God for the rest.

The earth is what we all have in common.

Wendell Berry

Get behind an effort you can feel passionate about. Your passion will help you stay engaged. Join with others who share your concerns, adding friendship and teamwork to the mix.

Fulfilling Your Destiny

*You and a friend are on a road trip, and you're lost. You think you
know which direction to go, but your friend insists the opposite
way is the one to take, so you do. With every mile you travel,
however, you feel more and more stressed out.*

For many people, life is like a road trip without a map. They sense that they're destined to be somewhere, but since they're not sure exactly where, they're not sure which road to take, and suggestions from others conflict with the direction they feel intuitively.

When you listen to the way God is leading your heart, you take the stress out of life's journey. Where your heart leads you is where your true destiny lies. Even though you may not understand every twist and turn along the way, you will know you are headed in the right direction as you continue to listen to God's voice leading you. No one but God knows your destiny better than you do, and it is your joy and privilege to fulfill it, wherever it may lead you.

Like a reliable road map, the Bible provides you with dependable directions as you travel your heart's route. The Bible is full of time-tested wisdom, unfailing promises, and Spirit-filled affirmations you can trust. You will discover that you are never traveling alone, but with God. God created you for a purpose, and he desires to see you fulfill what he has in mind for you. Knowing that, you can relax and enjoy every mile of the journey.

Top Ten Things to Do

10. Describe the destiny your heart desires.

9. List steps you are taking now to fulfill it.

8. Plan the next steps you will take.

7. Reject habits and attitudes not in accord with your destiny.

6. Focus on your destiny when making decisions and choices.

5. Consult God's guidance faithfully and frequently.

4. Embrace surprises and discoveries along the way.

3. Pray as you travel life's journey.

2. Enjoy the scenery along the way.

1. Believe in yourself and your destiny.

61 Let the Music Lift You

Music is God's gift to man, the only art of Heaven given to earth, the only art of earth we take to Heaven.

Walter Savage Landor

It's been a nerve-racking day with lots of stressors. You head for your car, dreading the long drive home and the many responsibilities waiting for you. You drag across the parking lot, get in your car and buckle up, turn on the ignition, and hit the Play button. Suddenly, the car is flooded with stress-relieving, mood-lifting tunes. Ahh. Soon you are singing along with your favorite CD, and by the time you get home, you're ready to tackle life again. That's the power of music.

Among the first things to happen when you listen to music is that you begin to breathe more deeply, your heart rate slows somewhat, your body begins to produce serotonin (a natural mood lifter), and your body temperature rises (an indication of the onset of relaxation). It isn't known exactly why our bodies respond to music as they do. Some researchers speculate that the rhythms and beats may remind us of the sound of a mother's heartbeat in the safety and warmth of the womb.

Thank God for music as you let it lift you up.

Try an invigorating "sound bath." Put on some relaxing music and lie in a comfortable position in a place where you can tune out everything but the music. For the next twenty minutes, let the music wash over you. If you are easily distracted, wear headphones.

Enjoy Special Scents

62

Close your eyes and imagine you're sitting peacefully in a beautiful, verdant garden. You're surrounded by tweeting songbirds, luscious blossoms, and fragrance—fragrance that transports you from the chaos of the day to the calm of your own private Eden.

Studies in aromatherapy have shown that certain fragrances help reduce cortisol levels in the body. Cortisol, a natural hormone produced when the body is under stress, becomes dangerous when levels remain high over time. In addition, fragrance has been shown to relax your body, enhance your mood, and relieve tension. As a part of your spiritual practice, a pleasing scent can help you focus your mind on God and lift you to a higher level of attentiveness.

Popular aromas for relaxation and cortisol reduction include lavender, jasmine, chamomile, basil, and ginger. You can find these pleasing scents in candles or as oils for use in a diffuser, as bath oil, or with other elements as a massage oil. Enjoy the peace, serenity, and health benefits that fragrances can add to your life.

Let my prayer be set before You as incense.

Psalm 141:2, NKJV

Before experimenting with therapeutic essential oils, consult a physician if you are pregnant or under treatment for epilepsy or hypertension. Discontinue use if a rash appears.

63 Cut Back on Caffeine and Sugar

It's midafternoon, and your body's in a slump. A soda, a cup of java, or a candy bar is just what you need to make it through the day. But the boost of alertness and energy comes at a cost, because by late afternoon you're left feeling fidgety, headachy, and nervous.

Too much caffeine and sugar is not only bad for your mood, it's also bad for your body. High levels of caffeine reduce your body's production of hormones that work to calm you and allow you to sleep comfortably at night. Caffeine also increases production of cortisol, the stress hormone, a cause of heart problems and other health issues. Excessive sugar in your diet brings few nutrients but lots of calories, leading to various physical and emotional problems, including diabetes, weight gain, chronic tension, and poor nutrition.

Both caffeine and sugar can be part of a healthy diet if they're enjoyed in moderation. Let nature's waker-upper and tasty treat keep your spirit genuinely vibrant and sweet.

Eat honey because it is good, and the honeycomb which is sweet to your taste.

Proverbs 24:13, NKJV

To avoid highs and lows in your energy level caused by too much caffeine and sugar, substitute water, fruit juice, herbal teas, and healthy snacks, especially in the afternoon and evening.

Shun Addictive Substances 64

Friday night is here at last, and you deserve to relax. Some people think there's nothing better for coming down from a long, stressful week than a few drinks, a couple of smokes, or a little pill or two.

While alcohol, tobacco, and drugs may pose as good tension relievers, these substances, without exception, open you to far more pressing problems than a demanding workweek. Substance abuse increases your risk of having or causing an accident, saying or doing things damaging to your reputation and relationships, suffering substance-related health issues, and even becoming involved in illegal activity. Now there's a real stressor.

God gave you the gift of free will, and with it he blessed you with the strength and power to opt for healthy and lasting stress-reduction strategies. When you need to get rid of stress and get rid of it now, make the decision that will leave you truly relaxed, refreshed, and reenergized. Choose what you can feel good about later as well as now.

Don't destroy yourself by getting drunk, but let the Spirit fill your life.

Ephesians 5:18, CEV

If you abuse substances to relieve stress, make a list of healthy alternatives, and post the list where you'll see it when tempted to go for the quick fix. Get help if you're unable to kick the habit by yourself.

65 Take Care of Business

Do your duty in all things. You cannot do more, you should never wish to do less.

Robert E. Lee

It's no fun going to the dentist for a checkup or spending money to get a drippy faucet fixed, and who can blame you for putting it off? Before you know it, however, you're living with a constant undercurrent of stress because you're aware that there are a number of important to-dos that aren't being done.

Make a list of things you tend to put off too long. Include appointments with health and other professionals, household repairs, yard upkeep, auto maintenance, and necessary purchases. Now prioritize each one, and commit to take care of one at a time over the course of a month, or longer if needed, until you have crossed off the last item. Then make a schedule so you can keep current throughout the year.

A balanced life includes time for business and time for fun, time for things of the world and time for things of the Spirit. Free yourself to enjoy the pleasurable and seek the spiritual by taking care of the business of the day.

Find a way to make your least favorite to-do item less of a chore by pairing it with something pleasurable, such as an eye-exam appointment with a visit to an ice-cream parlor or favorite coffee shop.

Drink Plenty of Water 66

Do you drink enough water? Most people don't. By some estimates, 75 percent of Americans are chronically dehydrated. The good news is that we live in a country that is blessed with a plentiful supply of clean, drinkable water.

Your body desperately needs water to keep your muscles and skin toned, carry oxygen and nutrients to your cells, eliminate toxins and waste, and regulate your body temperature. Without it, your body lacks what it needs to cushion your joints and protect your tissues and organs, including your spinal cord. Just a 2 percent drop in body water can cause light-headedness, confusion, and lack of focus.

You may be getting enough water to avoid extreme symptoms but not enough to keep you from feeling stressed and unable to relax. So drink up. Eight glasses a day of the cool, clear wonder should eliminate at least one source of your physical and mental stress and get your body and mind moving again.

Water is the most neglected nutrient in your diet, but one of the most vital.

Kelly Barton

If you find the taste of plain water boring, try one of the new water flavorings in the tea section of the grocery store, or simply add a little citrus juice to perk up the taste and keep you going back for more.

67

Clean Out a Closet

Yesterday's clothes landed in a heap on the closet floor because you were tired last night. This morning you were in a hurry, and you had to tear through a closet jam-packed with hangers looking for something to wear and then scramble to find matching shoes. Inside your closet, the view isn't pretty.

Imagine yourself opening your closet door and being greeted by clothes and shoes neatly arranged, sweaters carefully folded in clear plastic boxes, and an attractive hamper for your laundry. Doesn't that bring a relaxed smile to your face? An orderly closet isn't just for eye appeal, either. An orderly closet keeps your possessions properly stored and lets you easily find what you're looking for.

The LORD searches all hearts and understands every plan and thought.

1 Chronicles 28:9, ESV

What's inside counts in your spiritual life, too. Though no one can see what you have stored in your heart, you know what's there. Ask God to clean from your heart those things that cause you embarrassment, fear, anxiety, or regret. Clean closets and a clean heart can make a world of difference.

When deciding which clothes to keep and which to give away, don't base your judgment on the condition of the garment, but rather how long it's been since you last wore it. Generally speaking, if you haven't worn it for a year, let it go.

Evaluate Your Work Habits

68

It was a short report, and you figured you could get it done before lunch. But then a colleague stopped by to chat, and after she left, the telephone rang. After you hung up and worked a little more, you stopped to check your e-mail and your Facebook page. By the end of the day, the report wasn't finished, so you stayed late—again.

Studies have shown it will take you about fifteen minutes to get back on task after someone or something has broken your train of thought. Depending on your responsibilities, you may not be able to avoid interruptions, but you can take steps to reduce them. Discipline yourself to read and answer e-mail in the morning, after lunch, and at the end of the day. Ask friends not to call you while you're at work, and save casual conversations with coworkers for break time.

Staying on task requires discipline, but it is worth the trouble, for it pays off in the calm satisfaction you feel when you avoid stressful deadlines and unfinished projects.

Discipline is the bridge between goals and accomplishments.

Jim Rohn

If possible, post a schedule of times you are available to answer questions and assist others, and stick to the schedule. Screen the entry to your work space, or put a sign by the door.

69 Know You Can't Fix Everything

Tossing and turning, you were up all night trying to find a solution for someone who has made poor choices and is now in a fix. If you step back and look, you'll see that you are trying to carry someone else's responsibility, someone else's consequences, and in the process, someone else's stress. Don't you have enough stressors of your own?

If you want to be respected by others, the great thing is to respect yourself.

Fyodor Dostoyevsky

The fact that you want to help says you are a compassionate and caring person. But it may also say that you have a little mental glitch that makes you feel personally responsible for the happiness of others and guilty if you can't achieve that result.

The reality is that feeling responsible for everyone in every situation sets you up to fail. It just isn't possible, and it isn't supposed to be. When you hijack responsibility that belongs to others, you cheat them of the opportunity to work out their own solutions and learn from their experiences. Rest in this reassuring thought: if God needs your help, he'll ask for it. Now get some sleep.

When you find yourself listening to those embroiled in difficulties, it's fine to offer practical advice if you are able and you are asked. But do not feel you have to be the solution to that person's problem. Help if you wish, but reject the idea that you must.

Live within Your Means

70

Every shiny new model you see whizzing by on the road seems like a personal insult, and before you've gone another mile, you're feeling angry, tense, and resentful. You're still driving your ten-year-old clunker, and you're not happy about it.

Without doubt, living within your means requires you to stick to a budget and not buy things you can't afford. But peacefully and joyfully living within your means is something else again. This requires the God-given spiritual maturity to embrace the income you have right now without envying the income of others or resenting what others can afford to buy. Whether you have little or you have much, once you accept your own situation with gratitude, you will be surprised when you realize how rich you really are.

A contented spirit is true wealth and a great possession. Pray for the spiritual maturity it takes to live within your means in all ways, thanking God for all you have—old or new, big or small—and live bountifully.

Keep your lives free from the love of money, and be content with what you have.

Hebrews 13:5, NRSV

Get into the habit of saving by setting up a realistic savings plan, and deposit a predetermined amount into it with every paycheck. Making a regular contribution is more important than how much you put in.

71   Take an Interest in a Sports Team

Sports do not build character. They reveal it.

John Wooden

Why are people so caught up with sports? You've never understood it. You've attended a few games and watched people screaming and jumping around because a home run, touchdown, or field goal went their way. You've seen people dressed in team colors with painted faces high-fiving strangers. Whoa! It's just a game, right?

Well, kind of. It's a game, but while it lasts, those who join in receive the gift of several hours of nonstop physical and emotional release. When you, as an invested spectator, watch your favorite player flying down the ice and hooking the puck into the net, it's as if you were skating yourself. You are part of the action, part of the excitement, part of the win. It's glorious.

Sports will also remind you that whether you win or lose today, the sun will come up in the morning. And with the new day, God sends second chances and new beginnings. Defeat isn't permanent; life goes on. It's a lesson that will help you relax and take life less seriously.

❦

In order to benefit from the cathartic nature of sports, choose a specific sport and learn the rules. Then choose a team and get to know the players. Once you've bought in emotionally, you'll be able to lose yourself in the game.

Keep Your Work Skills Updated

72

Even though you're thankful you have a job, every rumor of a layoff, reorganization, or management change causes you to wonder: *Will I be next to get the ax?* While you used to enjoy what you do, now you walk into your workplace under a cloud of fear and tension.

Typically, the people who survive tough times are those who take control of their situations. If you are fortunate enough to have a job, keep your résumé updated. Your professional-looking résumé is a great confidence booster (yes, you did achieve all those things), and it comes in handy if an in-house job opens that you want to apply for. Employed or unemployed, enroll in classes—online or at a community college—and keep your skills fresh. Constantly look for ways to broaden your field of expertise.

The purpose of learning is growth, and our minds, unlike our bodies, can continue growing as long as we live.

Mortimer Adler

You can't prevent change, but you can be prepared for it. And whatever happens, you can rely on God, who never changes in his desire to bless your life. With your trust placed firmly in him, you can look forward to every day with confidence.

Many employers will pay tuition and allow time off for their employees to take classes that will enhance their work skills. It never hurts to ask if this is the case where you work. Even if it isn't, bringing it up might cause your employer to consider it.

Money Matters

No matter where you fall on the socioeconomic scale, you have almost certainly found that money and anxiety go hand in hand. Only when you've come to grips with the financial issues of life will you be able to relax and live in contentment with what God has given you.

People who don't have enough money typically think their troubles would be over if only they had more of the green stuff. But if you ask any lottery winner, you are likely to find that having too much money has a sharp edge of its own. On both ends of the spectrum, money matters are major stressors. In fact, most people spend their days either pursuing money, managing it, or repairing the damage it has caused. Where can you find a point of peace?

Look to the life of Jesus for an example. We know he didn't dismiss money, because his little band of disciples had a treasurer. We also know that he didn't covet it, because he had very few personal possessions and never asked for money from those who followed him. Instead, it would seem that Jesus saw money simply as a tool, something used to pay taxes and procure necessary resources.

What is your philosophy concerning money? Do you feel your life would be enhanced by wealth? How much does your attitude about money factor into your stress level? Ask yourself these questions, and then prayerfully ask God to help you find the critical balance money matters should have in your life. Ask him to help you bring back the peace.

Top Ten Things to Do

10. Assess your attitude toward money.

9. Compare your monthly income and expenditures.

8. Commit to a realistic budget.

7. Share a percentage of your income with others.

6. Save a percentage of your income for emergencies.

5. Think before you make purchases.

4. Avoid credit card debt and unnecessary loans.

3. Be content with what you have.

2. Find creative ways to reuse and recycle.

1. Trust in God, not in money.

73

Be Realistic about Time

It took twenty minutes to get ready for your appointment, but you allotted only ten minutes. You thought you could make up the lost time on your drive across town, but that took longer than you expected as well. Now you are really sweating it, and you're going to show up significantly late.

Chronic lateness is not so much a problem of careless disregard as it is unrealistic time management. It is a common problem with serious consequences—blown meetings, canceled appointments, and missed flights, to name a few—but there is an easy fix.

On a day when you are not in a hurry to get somewhere, pay attention to how long it takes you to shower and dress in a relaxed manner. Add ten minutes, and you have a good estimation of how much time you need to get ready. Time a test drive to work, the airport, the doctor's office, and other frequent destinations. Add ten minutes, and you'll eliminate the tardiness stressor from your life.

Punctuality is a sign of respect—both for you and for others.

Joan Gamble

Start time is critical. When you have to be somewhere at a certain time, count back from the desired arrival time, accounting for drive time, preparation time, and an extra ten minutes for unexpected interruptions, and you will have your start time.

Pace Yourself

74

This was the day to plant your spring garden. At least you thought it was. But now you're overwhelmed and stressed out. It's too bad because you usually enjoy your gardening duties. Maybe it's time to step back and remind yourself that God has given you the gift of time; everything doesn't have to happen today.

It's easy to let your initial enthusiasm for a project cause you to get in over your head. When you do, stress you don't want or need replaces the fun you should be having. To avoid this situation, it's always best to begin with a plan. Before starting any project, put down on paper the steps needed, and break the project down into parts you can easily manage. When that's done, get out your calendar (the one with your current obligations and appointments) and start fitting the tasks required into your schedule.

When you tackle projects at a manageable pace, you will alleviate stress and give yourself space to enjoy what you're doing and give it your best effort.

A good plan is like a road map: it shows the final destination and usually the best way to get there.

H. Stanley Judd

Some projects require more planning and expertise than others. Most home-improvement stores have pros on hand who are happy to answer questions and help you with the planning, cost estimating, and execution of your project.

75

Insist on Some Alone Time

Care for some company?" Actually, you were looking forward to taking a leisurely walk by yourself, but you smile politely and say, "Sure, come along." Though your companions are nice to be with, you know you won't get the stress-relieving quiet time you were hoping for.

Inside myself is a place where I live all alone, and that's where you renew your springs that never dry up.

Pearl S. Buck

Every day, you need some time by yourself to think, meditate, and pray. Alone, you can become more attuned to your thoughts, emotions, and surroundings; you can gain insight, solve problems, and de-stress your body and soul. Taking this alone time is one of the nicest things you can do for those around you, too. When you're relaxed and together, you swing the equation toward peace and away from chaos.

You need not waste a moment feeling guilty about protecting your time alone. The next time someone asks to come along, smile politely and say, "That's a difficult offer to resist. You know how I love spending time with you. But believe me, it's best for both of us if I use this time to get my head on straight."

Avoid awkward situations by casually communicating to your family and friends how much you enjoy your time alone every day and how you believe it benefits you. Urge them to take some time alone for themselves as well.

Count Your Blessings

76

At the end of a long, hard day, you're wondering how you're going to make it through the evening. What can you do to pep yourself up? Though it may sound simplistic, one of the best things you can do to revive yourself is to count your blessings.

Begin by naming your family members, friends, and all your favorite things, but don't stop there. Think of blessings so often taken for granted, like your ability to breathe, smile, and laugh; to think, feel, love, imagine, dream, discover, and be the unique human being you are.

God has richly blessed you in many ways. Think of the gift of your life. Give special thanks for something you see every day, like the tree budding outside your window or the clouds scooting across the sky. Count simple and common things, like a cozy chair and your fuzzy warm slippers. Once you start counting your blessings, you won't know when to stop. As for your stress? What stress?

O taste and see that the
Lord is good.

Psalm 34:8, NRSV

Before you go to sleep, name five specific blessings unique
to that day. Describe to yourself what made these blessings
special, and give God thanks for each one.

99

77 Learn How to Relax Your Body

Ouch. After hours at the computer, your aching shoulders yearn for relief. After a long car trip, your back begs for movement. After an afternoon digging in the garden, your knees let you know you've done too much. You're not being punished for working hard; you're simply experiencing your body's natural vulnerability.

When you sit or stand for long periods of time, tension builds up in muscles and joints, causing pain and inflammation. A good way to relieve stress buildup is to consciously relax by focusing on each particular part of your body for a few moments, mentally instructing your face, neck, shoulders, torso, back, legs, knees, and feet to relax as you go from head to toe. Give special attention to unusually achy areas.

Your body is God's gift to you, and it is marvelously made. Use it, enjoy it, and praise him for it. At the end of each day, treat your body to the relaxation it needs.

I will praise You, for I am fearfully and wonderfully made.

Psalm 139:14, NKJV

If you work at a desk or computer all day, take a short break about once an hour. Walk down the hall and back, circle your desk, or just stretch and twist where you are. This allows you to release tension periodically rather than letting it build to a critical point.

Dream Big Dreams

78

In a moment of repose, you find yourself thinking back over your life, remembering a time long gone when everything seemed possible. You weren't afraid to dream big dreams back then. But now you feel the need to behave as an adult, be responsible, and deal with the realities of life.

While reality checks are good and a necessary part of being successful, it takes dreams and the ability to continue dreaming to creatively change and shape reality. Dreaming allows you to invent new pathways, attempt new things, and revise the ways you do things. Dreams express the desires of your heart, desires that may be the whisper of God's Spirit telling you what's possible and what's achievable. You might say they are the seeds of God's plans for you.

What do you remember dreaming about when you were small? Does it make you smile now, or laugh, or wonder what if? No matter how old you are, let yourself revisit those big dreams and relax in the glory of life as it could be.

You can often measure a person by the size of his dream.

Robert H. Schuller

Choose one thing you always dreamed about doing. Perform some research and then write a plan for making that dream become a reality. Most dreams are more easily attainable than you might think.

79

Cook for the Joy of It

It's been a long, stressful week, and you're tempted to sit on the sofa and watch the weekend slip away. Then a thought crosses your mind—brownies, chocolate-chip cookies, or fettuccini Alfredo. Just like that, your inner battery gets a jump start.

Since the Garden of Eden, God has given man food for both nourishment and pleasure. Cooking with all its inviting tastes and aromas can truly be a balm to a troubled soul. Something as simple as adding a new spice or flavoring to an old recipe or throwing something yummy on the grill can energize you and help you forget the extremities of the week behind you.

There's more to cooking than just getting a meal on the table. Take your time, and produce a creation you can be proud of. Try something new that will challenge and intrigue you. Cooking can be a sensuous activity, especially when you share what you cook with those you love.

The eyes of all look to you, and you give them their food in due season.

Psalm 145:15, ESV

Sit down with a good cookbook and read some of the recipes. Linger over the photographs, and imagine how each dish will taste and smell. When you find just the right one, go for it—it will be great fun.

Get a Physical

80

Lately you haven't had the energy to do the things you'd like to do. It's nothing you can put your finger on, but you feel dragged out most of the time. Yes, stress will do that to you, but some health issues will, too.

If it's been a year or more since you've had a complete physical, perhaps it's time to make an appointment with your physician. While your less-than-peak energy level may be due to stress, it could also be caused by something else entirely. The same can be said of muscle tension—it might stem from the way you're standing or sitting, but it's good to know for sure. A professional medical opinion will put your mind at ease, which will reduce your stress about it and encourage you to start on a medication or exercise plan, if needed.

One way to say thank you to God for the gift of your body is to do your part to keep it operating efficiently.

Don't you know that you yourselves are God's temple and that God's Spirit lives in you?

1 Corinthians 3:16, NIV

Prepare for your visit with your physician by making a list of the changes you've noticed in your health, along with the name and dosage of all over-the-counter and prescription medicines you take.

81   Do Something You Enjoy

I want to do it because I want to do it.

Amelia Earhart

Tamping down the dirt around your prize rosebush, you inhale aromas of earth and blossom. Your fingers fly over the piano keys, engaging mind and body. The cares of the world fall away as you put brush to canvas, reveling in the solid lines and vibrant colors. Doing what you love to do quiets and revives you. It provides an escape and a way to re-energize.

Maybe you enjoy jogging in your neighborhood or working out at the gym. Perhaps you're a crossword-puzzle enthusiast or a reader of good books. For everyone there is something, and when you are engaged in that something, your muscles relax and tension melts away. For that little while, you are in harmony with your innermost self.

Call them what you will—talents, proclivities, hobbies, pastimes—they are natural stress relievers. Whether you prefer origami, woodworking, or martial arts, find what you love and let it take you to your special stress-free zone.

In the crush of responsibilities and demands on your time, it is understandable to feel guilty about taking time for what you love. Remind yourself of the benefits, and give yourself permission to engage your passion at least once or twice a week.

Refuse to Be a Martyr

82

It's one of those days, and you can't help thinking everyone wants a piece of you. No one seems to care what you want or need. Just the same, you push down the growing resentment and continue to carry the load others have piled on your shoulders. You've chosen to be a martyr. That's right. Chosen.

It's a common thing, especially for caregivers, to begin to find identity in the role of martyr. It becomes a form of unhealthy self-esteem. Meanwhile, troubled waters lie under the surface. Tension and stress can grow to extreme levels. If you find yourself in this situation, you must recognize that you have chosen the role you are in, and only you can choose to change it. You must meet your responsibilities, of course, but insisting on meeting the unreasonable demands of others while sacrificing your own needs should not be part of the bargain.

Treat yourself with respect and dignity, and gently and politely make it clear that you expect others to do the same.

Never grow a wishbone, daughter, where a backbone ought to be.

Clementine Paddleford

Make this simple rule a part of every day: Don't do for others what they can and should do for themselves. It will help you make better choices for yourself.

83 Take Up Gardening

Checking out at your local home-improvement store, you spot a display next to the register. Little seed packets of promise, the hope of coming spring; you find yourself staring. Carrots, tomatoes, and look at all those beautiful flowers. You wish you had your neighbor's green thumb.

Green thumb or not, gardening is for everyone. Who wouldn't find it relaxing to be in the company of little green sprouts, newly opened blossoms, tender new branches, and rich dark earth. Gardening is a natural de-stressor. It connects you with God's good creation and lets you experience the natural seasons of life and growth.

The key is not to bite off more than you can chew. If you're a beginner, choose a small, easily maintained project. As you get the hang of it, you can always add to your gardening experience. The point is, slow down—lose yourself in the primal feel and smell of the soil and the reward of God's promised harvest.

Buy a potted plant or an outdoor shrub or tree you have never worked with before. In a notebook, write your observations as you tend the plant through every season of the year.

The LORD God planted a garden in Eden, in the east, and there he put the man whom he had formed.

Genesis 2:8, ESV

Keep a Check on Your Attitude 84

The person at the next table is bellyaching about how bad things are and is going on and on about why this, why that, why me. Annoyed, you shake your head and try to shut out the whiner. At the same time, however, you ask yourself, *Do I sound like that?*

In everyone's life, God permits problems to arise, bad circumstances to exist, and adversity to strike. He also allows individuals the freedom to choose how to handle these things. To those who ask, God gives the power to meet life's challenges with his power—the power of hope, trust, and reliance on him. And with power like that, a positive attitude naturally flows. You know that you will come through, things will work out, and God will provide the solution.

Attitude is everything, especially when nothing seems to be going right. You can focus on the problems and all the stress that comes with them, or you can bring your problems to God, and in his peace, discover his answers.

Blessed are the people whose God is the LORD.

Psalm 144:15, NIV

Flip problems by asking yourself what good could come from the situation you are facing. Will it make you wiser, stronger, more confident? Focusing on the possible redemption in each problem can improve your attitude.

Setting Boundaries

It feels good to be the go-to person everyone depends on for assistance and advice. Then it happens: people expect you to drop what you're doing, come right over, listen to them complain, and solve their problems. It's time to set boundaries.

In a sincere desire to serve others, many people make it a priority to become an integral part of their community. They are the ones who always get the work done and keep things running smoothly. In families, they're the devoted parents and caregivers, and they're the ones their friends know they can call on, day or night. A laudable lifestyle, however, turns stressful and overwhelming when no personal boundaries prevent others from taking advantage of one's generosity.

When you're accustomed to meeting the expectations of others, you may feel uncomfortable setting personal boundaries. Yet your just, fair, and reasonable boundaries keep stress and resentment out of your unselfish lifestyle. Boundaries simply keep others aware that you need time to rest, relax, and refresh, and God expects you to tend to those needs so you have the strength and motivation to continue to reach out.

When you set boundaries, you are actually positioning yourself to serve others more effectively and productively. You will be able to give the things you choose to do your full time and attention. With boundaries in place, you have time to pursue your own interests, which will help you continue to be the kind, generous, and compassionate person you are.

Top Ten Things to Do

10. Reclaim your time as your own to control.

9. Identify requests and obligations that cause you stress.

8. Delegate wherever possible and appropriate.

7. Practice saying no to unreasonable requests.

6. Commit to your own physical and spiritual needs.

5. Make time for you a daily priority.

4. Reject the idea that you can please everyone.

3. Remain firm on the boundaries you set.

2. Avoid people who take advantage of you.

1. Take care of yourself so you can better serve others.

85 Monitor Your Physical Health

*Health is the thing
that makes you feel
that now is the best
time of the year.*

Franklin Pierce Adams

Perhaps you've been healthy all your life. You've never had to think twice about what you choose to eat or drink. Your fast metabolism has provided plenty of energy and kept you slender. You can't imagine that changing, but you might be surprised.

With every candle on your birthday cake, your health needs change because your body changes. Five years ago, you may not have needed to check your cholesterol level, but maybe now you do. It's possible that a fix for your present complaint of nervousness could be something as simple as taking a vitamin supplement every day. Screenings and tests, as advised by a health professional, catch problems early and prevent serious health issues.

A checkup on your spiritual health might be in order, too, because a troubled, uneasy spirit can bring on very real physical symptoms. Do you feel at peace in your relationship with God? Do your family, friends, and activities bring you genuine refreshment and joy? Be responsible about your physical—and spiritual—health.

*Find out when your area hospital or health department holds
free health fairs or offers screenings open to the community.
Mark the date on your calendar, and get your basic tests done.*

Know Your Limitations

86

Wow, you can do everything," your friend gushes. The admiration you earn from others by being a corporate manager, an up-and-comer in your field, a genial host, and the volunteer of the year is a real ego-booster. It's only the stress that gets you down.

Already you have discovered that keeping a full calendar is not the same as living a full life. Sure, you can cram in another committee meeting, but at what cost? Another evening away from your family? Another movie night missed and another weekend spent in front of the computer? The stress you feel is your body's way of telling you it's time to embrace your limitations. When you acknowledge and obey your limitations, you can give your work your best effort and still have time for refreshment and relaxation with family and friends.

God gave each person different and unique abilities and talents. Never does he expect anyone to do everything, including you. Embrace your limitations so you can genuinely enjoy the boundless delight of life.

There are diversities of gifts, but the same Spirit.

1 Corinthians 12:4, NKJV

Change your role model from someone who seems to do everything to someone you know whose life appears balanced, stress-free, and joyful. Talk to the person about his or her choices.

87

Become a Patron of the Arts

*Praise the LORD
with the harp; make
melody to Him with
an instrument
of ten strings.*

Psalm 33:2, NKJV

It's been a long week, and by Friday afternoon you're exhausted. Then you glance at your calendar and realize it's concert night. You'd rather go home, relax, take a long, hot bath, and curl up with a good book. You wonder if one of your coworkers would like to have your ticket.

Before you decide against going, think about how the concert could provide you with an evening's relaxation, enjoyment, and relief from the stress of the day. The arts—concerts, museums, plays, opera, dance, and song—are where you can find inspiration, entertainment, and life enrichment. Soaring music lifts your spirit to other worlds of feeling and emotion; thought-provoking plays probe the essence of religion, relationships, and life; comedy and lighthearted shows keep you laughing all the way home.

For a few hours of much-needed relief, keep that concert ticket. You'll wonder why it ever crossed your mind to give that ticket away. Plan to spend leisurely afternoons in your local museum and attend live performances frequently.

*Invite a friend to join you for an afternoon or evening at a
concert or other live performance in your community. After
the event, share your feelings, thoughts, and discoveries.*

Try Something New

88

Nothing ever changes, you complain to a friend. You're in a funk. Your same old routine is comfortable but boring, and boredom breeds depression, fatigue, and stress. Doing something you've never done before can seem a little daunting, but when you wade into the water, you could find yourself invigorated and enjoying a new lease on life.

You don't need to move to another city or change careers. Trying something new can be as simple as driving a different route on your way to work or riding a bus or bicycle instead of driving. You could take up conversational Italian through an adult education program or learn how to play table tennis. So what if you're not too good at it? You won't be great at everything you try, but no one cares. No one is keeping score.

An endless number of brand-new adventures await you. All you need is a willingness to do a little research and the courage to step out of your comfort zone.

The one who was seated on the throne said, "See, I am making all things new."

Revelation 21:5, NRSV

Pick up a copy of the class schedule for your local community college. Most of these schools carry classes in everything from sign language to belly dancing to auto mechanics. Find a few minutes to look it over and see if anything strikes your fancy.

89

Learn to Dance

Everything in the universe has rhythm. Everything dances.

Maya Angelou

Hate exercise? Maybe, but you know you need to do it more often. It's boring doing the same old bends, stretches, and push-ups. Why not try dancing instead? Dancing is a great way to get in touch with your body, reduce stress, increase agility, and meet fun and interesting people.

Like an exercise regimen, dance gets you off the couch, moving around, and loosening tense joints and muscles. Unlike exercise, however, dance teaches you how to express yourself through movement as you study its traditional forms or revel in free-form contemporary styles. With music as your constant partner, you'll not only feel the rhythm, you'll also de-stress to it.

Some churches open their doors to liturgical dancing, that is, dance movement in response to God's presence, his creation, and other sacred themes. Try this: instead of saying a prayer today, dance a prayer in gratitude for the gift of music and movement. You could find yourself refreshed in body, soul, and spirit.

Get a group of your friends together, put on some music, and spend an evening teaching one another the dances you know and enjoy, even if no one has danced since high school.

114

Spend More Time Outdoors

90

All day you've been indoors, and you would love to get outside a little, but there's still work to do. You rub the back of your neck, hoping to relieve the stress that's built up during the day, glance at the sky through the window, and take up your next task. Sigh.

Studies have shown that even fifteen minutes outdoors each day in the fresh air can significantly lower your stress level. Taking a few deep breaths of fresh air clears the mind and gives you a quick shot of energy. Looking at the sky, the trees, the grass, and the flowers breaks you away from the deadening routine of eating, working, and sleeping. Listening to the wind and birdsong lifts your spirit to the wonders and beauty of God's good creation.

You might go to many places to find refreshment, rest, and relaxation, but one of the best is right outside your door. It's easy to get to, and it's free all day, every day.

The whole earth is filled with his glory!

Isaiah 6:3, NLT

Go outside and look around for a spot in your garden or in a nearby park that you find serene and peaceful. In a notebook, describe the place and your feelings when you are there.

91

Be Prepared

All the people rejoiced because God had prepared for the people, for the thing came about suddenly.

2 Chronicles 29:36, ESV

It didn't seem necessary to buy extra groceries or fill up the car with gas. After all, you had a lot to do, and you decided those things could wait until the weekend. Sure, a big snowstorm was in the forecast, but last time it never materialized, so you gave it little thought. Unfortunately, this time the storm roared in, and you found yourself in a tight spot.

The motto "Be prepared" isn't just for Scouts. Emergency situations are stressful, but the more prepared you are, the more calmly and effectively you can handle them. Indeed, a measure of preparedness may be all it takes to avoid an emergency, or take you from being the one in need of help to being the one able to help others.

Spiritual preparedness is also important. It equips your heart and mind to trust in God in all situations. It gives you the inner strength to rise above the extremities of your life and react with confidence, composure, and even humor.

From a health-care professional or a reliable Web site, get a list of basic medical supplies you should have in your home. Put these supplies in a box, and store it in a convenient and accessible place.

Be True to Who You Are

92

Like an actor in a role, lately you've become dissatisfied with the lines your role requires. You're dealing with the tension of trying to keep up appearances and the fear of someone peering behind the mask you're wearing. The gap between your role and your authentic self is a source of monumental stress.

With honest self-examination and a commitment to acting on what you discover, you can close the gap between the person you are presenting to the world and the person you really are. First, accept yourself fully, warts and all. Second, name your talents and achievements, and be proud of them; never gloss over your successes. Third, believe in yourself as someone God created to touch the lives of others by thinking, speaking, and acting from the heart.

God's Spirit lives in you, and you have no need to be ashamed of where you come from, what you do, or who you are. Peace is yours when you live as 100 percent you, through and through.

Identify the things you think, say, and do that are not, or are no longer, true to who you are. List three steps you can take to move toward greater authenticity and self-confidence.

Why do you pretend to be another person?

1 Kings 14:6, NKJV

93

Cry a Little

Tears well up in your eyes, but you quickly shake them off. You've always been told crying is a sign of weakness or melodrama. Nonsense. While there is clearly a time and place for crying, it is, in fact, a natural bodily response to pent-up emotion and anxiety.

Rejoice with those who rejoice, and weep with those who weep.

Romans 12:15, NKJV

When you are experiencing significant amounts of emotional stress, toxic chemicals build up in your body. Unlike tears caused by eye irritants, emotional tears have been shown to contain abundant amounts of adrenaline and other stress-related chemicals. Crying literally allows your body to sweep those dangerous toxins out and away. But the healthy benefits of your crying don't end there. As your tears are clearing away the toxins, they are also releasing many protein-based hormones, such as leucine enkephalin (a natural painkiller), prolactin, and the adrenocorticotropic hormone, which have been shown to reduce the buildup of stress.

When you're feeling tight and out of sorts, give yourself permission to let your tear ducts do the work God intended.

Designate a place for crying, somewhere out of the way so your tears won't perturb others. Don't wait until your stress level is at the breaking point. Go to your special place regularly, and let your tears clear your head.

Go for a Drive

94

A lot of time is spent in your car, going back and forth to work, ferrying your children to school and other activities, running errands. Driving is a necessity, but have you considered that it can also be a great stress reliever?

During the 1950s and 1960s, it was customary for the family to pile into the car on Sunday after church and go for a leisurely drive simply for the pleasure of watching the scenery go by, being together, and perhaps happening on a new picnic place or lookout point. In these times of frenetic activity and topped-out gas prices, however, we seem to have forgotten how relaxing and therapeutic a drive can be. You might say it allows you the freedom and opportunity to take a mini-vacation just by buckling up and heading away from the house.

When you're feeling stressed out, boxed in, and short on options, a change of scenery helps you get things into perspective. On any day of the week, there's nothing like a Sunday drive, just for the wonder of it.

I travel not to go anywhere, but to go. I travel for travel's sake. The great affair is to move.

Robert Louis Stevenson

Lay out a map of where you live and its environs. With your neighborhood as the center, draw a circle enclosing everything within a one-hundred-mile radius. Plan day trips to nearby points of interest.

95

Treat Yourself to a Massage

Your shoulder muscles are so tight you can't begin to loosen them up, and your neck feels as taut as twisted rope. There have been gray skies all week, and nothing you can think of to do is appealing. If this describes you, a massage may be just the thing to melt your stress away and pull your spirit out of the doldrums.

Taking care of your body isn't all about eating right and getting timely medical care. It's also about doing things designed to relieve physical tension and the spiritual stress of boredom and gloominess. An hour or so spent relaxing in serene surroundings under the trained hands of a professional masseuse or masseur will greatly improve your outlook on life.

The bliss e'en of a moment still is bliss.

Joanna Baillie

During your massage, get in touch with touch. Meditate on the miracle of your shoulders, arms, back, and legs. Thank God for each part of your body as the masseuse or masseur kneads and presses. The skies outside may still be gray, but you'll feel bathed in sunshine.

A professional masseuse or masseur may work in a beauty salon or day spa, at home, or in a medical setting. The best way to find a good one is to ask around. Like a good hairstylist, a good masseuse will have plenty of people singing his or her praises.

Pay Bills on Time

96

Oh, no, not again. The due date for payment on your charge card is tomorrow, and you forgot to mail your check. You know the routine: a scribbled check with an uneasy eye on the balance left in your account, a dash to the post office, a half hour spent standing in line, a charge for overnight delivery—phew. This is the kind of stress you can do without.

You can eliminate the hassle of last-minute bill paying (and potential late charges) by paying your bills on time. Find a convenient spot for all bills to go as you receive them. Once a week, go through the bills and pay those that are due within the next ten days. That way, you will never need to panic at the sight of a missed due date.

Remaining current on bills is more than just a way to maintain a healthy credit score. It is also a way of honoring God by expressing integrity, honesty, and trustworthiness in all things.

Those who borrow are slaves of moneylenders.

Proverbs 22:7, CEV

It's more difficult to keep track of your bills when their due dates are strung out randomly throughout the month. Arrange for the due dates to fall into two groups: one at the beginning and one at the middle of the month.

Finding the Balance

*You probably know how to work hard. But do you know how to play
hard, too? Many people who work hard find little time or energy left
over for play, yet a balance of work and play is essential for physical
and emotional well-being. The one needs the other.*

After a hard day's work, your body and mind need an opportunity to unwind. Taking time to do something you find relaxing and enjoyable allows you to release the day's pent-up stress and tension. A brisk walk, an hour at the gym, working a crossword puzzle, teaching your dog a few new tricks—these activities relax your muscles and help clear your head.

In the Bible, God declared one day each week as a day of rest. God's action serves to emphasize the need for balance in life between work and play. A life that is all work leads to stress, burnout, and the inability to work effectively and productively. All work causes life to become rigid and lacking in creativity. All play, on the other hand, eventually makes life seem meaningless and bereft of joy. God, in his care for you, would have you avoid both extremes.

Along with a good day's work, allow yourself a guilt-free time to play, and give play your whole heart. The hour you spend in play will reward you with reduced stress, better health, and a sense of well-being. When you're ready to get back to work, don't be surprised if you find your work sparkles a little more brightly as well.

Top Ten Things to Do

10. Find something fun you can do each day.

9. Reserve time each day for fun.

8. Avoid spending long hours at work.

7. Analyze how you spend your time.

6. Leave work at work, even if you work at home.

5. Keep playtimes work-free and distraction-free.

4. Arrange days off from chores as often as possible.

3. Drop optional activities you don't really enjoy.

2. Manage your time wisely every day.

1. Set aside time to worship, meditate, and pray.

97

Stick with the Truth

Maybe you thought the little fib on your social-networking page would add a bit of spark to your profile. Who would know the difference, anyway? Yet in all likelihood, your long-time friends will notice the deception immediately, and your new friends will uncover it soon enough. You'll end up looking silly or dishonest.

In the virtual world, it can be tempting to refashion yourself as more accomplished, more attractive, or more adventurous than you really are. A little exaggeration here and there may seem like harmless fun at first, but it erodes your credibility as a person and creates an unhealthy inner conflict. It's easy to see, too, how the habit of giving out little lies now can open the door to other, more-substantial false stories later.

In the virtual world, and definitely in the real world, it's best to stick with the truth. You'll sleep better at night and be more relaxed during the day.

Honesty guides good people.

Proverbs 11:3, NLT

Scan your résumé and your social-networking sites for information that is exaggerated, embellished, or misleading. Delete it, or reword the information to more accurately reflect the truth.

Keep Your Conscience Clear

98

Even though it happened years ago, possibly decades ago, it still troubles you. That was the day you—well, fill in the blank. For all this time, it has been on your conscience, and whenever you're reminded of it, you're filled with embarrassment, shame, tension, and regret.

Part of the adventure of living is making mistakes, and some of those mistakes weigh heavily on the conscience for a long time. You would apologize and make amends if you were able, but the opportunity has long passed. If you could do it all over again, you would behave differently, but what's done cannot be undone.

To relieve your conscience, put your faith in God's desire and willingness to forgive you. Then forgive yourself. Lift it off your conscience, and let its memory serve as a gentle reminder that doing the right thing, the honest thing, the trustworthy thing is the only route to a clear, unburdened conscience.

Create in me a clean heart, O God, and put a new and right spirit within me.

Psalm 51:10, NRSV

Make a habit of pausing to consider the potential consequences of a certain behavior before you engage in it. Acting on impulse is sure to get you in trouble.

99

Trust Your Kids to Parent

Children's children are a crown to the aged, and parents are the pride of their children.

Proverbs 17:6, NIV

Do you remember what your grandmother said about the clothes you wore in junior high? or about the age you were when your parents let you start dating? No doubt, your grandmother thought she was doing her duty by telling your mother what she ought to be doing to raise you right. But that's a surefire recipe for cross-generational stress.

When your children have children, it's hard not to revert to child-raising mode. You believe you know what they should be doing, and it may be true that you do. Nonetheless, it's the child you raised who has the child-raising responsibilities now. Trust his or her judgment. Believe in his or her abilities. Support your adult children as they take on the toughest job life will ever hand them.

Give thanks to God, for he has blessed you with the gift of family. Relax and enjoy the joyful job you have now, that of being a loving, supportive, grateful, and godly grandparent.

Focus on specific things your adult children are doing right in raising their children, and make a special effort to let them know you notice and appreciate the job they are doing. Be generous with encouragement and praise.

Keep an Open Mind

100

It struck you like a personal attack. A longtime friend started on about something you feel strongly about, and your blood pressure reached the boiling point before the two of you angrily parted ways. Days later, you still haven't calmed down.

An open mind doesn't mean that you agree with everything you hear, that you dilute your own values in favor of someone else's, or that you never offer a reasoned counterargument on a subject you feel strongly about. It does mean, however, that you listen to others with understanding and compassion and that you carefully consider their points of view. An open mind means you are open to changing your mind if the facts demand it.

Early Christian congregations were urged to listen and weigh everything they heard, and accept only what proved to be true in light of God's values and principles. This is the kind of open mind that God wants for you, an open mind that brings understanding, wisdom, confidence, and peace.

Test everything; hold fast what is good.

1 Thessalonians 5:21, ESV

When someone else's point of view evokes undue tension, breathe deeply and hear the person out before responding. Whenever possible, find points of agreement before addressing points of conflict.

*We are pressed on every side by troubles, but we
are not crushed. We are perplexed, but not driven to despair.*

2 Corinthians 4:8, NLT

*Stress is the trash of modern life—we all generate it,
but if you don't dispose of it properly, it will
pile up and overtake your life.*

Terri Guillemets

*Releasing the pressure, it's good for the
teapot and the water. Try it sometime.*

Jeb Dickerson

*Sometimes the most important thing in a
whole day is the rest we take between two deep breaths.*

Etty Hillesum

*When doubts filled my mind, your comfort
gave me renewed hope and cheer.*

Psalm 94:19, NLT